GHOSTBUSTERS™

THE OFFICIAL COOKBOOK

GHOSTBUSTERS™

THE OFFICIAL COOKBOOK

RECIPES BY JENN FUJIKAWA

WRITTEN BY ERIK BURNHAM

INSIGHT
EDITIONS

SAN RAFAEL · LOS ANGELES · LONDON

CONTENTS

DIETARY CONSIDERATIONS

GF = Gluten Free | V = Vegetarian | V+ = Vegan

Podcast's Marshmallow Fondue **GF**

Egon's Spores, Molds, and Fungus Stuffed Mushrooms **V**

Dana's Demon Eggs **GF, V**

Venkman Burn in Hell-apeño Poppers **GF, V**

Petty Cash Egg Rolls

Louis's Party Brie **GF, V**

Egon, Your Guacamole **GF, V, V+**

Farmhouse French Onion Soup

Interdimensional Cross-Rip Dip **GF, V**

Shandor Mining Company Pull-Apart Bread **V**

Firehouse Chili on the Go **GF**

Terror Dogs

Janine's World's Fair Falafel **V, V+**

Three Mortgage Soup **GF**

Kung Pao Shrimp

Spinners' Seismic Burger

Callie's Quesadillas

Phoebe's Pizza Puzzle **V**

Trevor's Grease Bomb Patty Melt

Summerville (Rust City) Chicken Fried Steak

How to Make an Edible Mini-Puft **GF**

Ghostbustin' Sweet Potatoes **GF**

Louis's Nutritious Quinoa Salad **GF, V, V+**

Yes, Have Some Ambrosia **GF**

Ugly Little Spuds **GF, V, V+**

Ghostbusters Super Diet Salad **GF**

Spinners' Loaded Onion Rings

Egon's Favorite Mac and Cheese **V**

Toasted Marshmallow Skewers **GF**

Slimer Salad **GF**

That's a Big Twinkie

Lucky's Donuts **V**

You've Earned It Candy Bar **V**

Muncher Cookies

Camp Waconda S'Mores Cookies

Dirt Farm Trap Pudding Cups **V**

Mr. Grooberson's Nightmare
Ice Cream Sundae

Psychomagnotheric Slime-Filled
Toaster Tarts **V**

Phoebe's Spectral Cheeseboard Cake **V**

Bug Eye Ghost Blackberry Tarts **V**

Mini-Puft Hot Cocoa **GF**

Gozer's Cotton Candy Cooler **GF, V, V+**

Ecto Juice **GF, V, V+**

The Keymaster's Peanut Butter Parallel **GF, V**

The Gatekeeper's Strawberry
Similarity **GF, V**

Class 5 Free-Roaming Vapor
Cider **GF, V, V+**

Matcha Milk Slimer **GF, V, V+**

Date Night Boba Fizz **GF, V, V+**

Zeddemore Executive Coffee **GF, V**

Podcast's Summerville Freeze **GF, V, V+**

FOREWORD

You never know what little thing is going to become important to your life. For me? I answered a crazy want ad on a whim. I didn't know I'd get the job, and I didn't know how that job would change me.

. . . But let me tell you, after you've saved the world (more than once), you won't be the same kind of person. You can't be.

I started a company, I started a family, and I found a lot of success in this world. And I owe all that to a confidence I might never have had without my experiences as a Ghostbuster. No matter who else I may become, I will always be a Ghostbuster. And as such, I want the memory of the Ghostbusters to be strong in the hearts and minds of the public.

Which brings me to this book.

As fellow Ghostbuster Peter Venkman once said, "The road to peoples' hearts is paved in merchandise."

That's when I got a call from Ray Stantz.

He'd found the remains of a project in storage—a cookbook, of all things. Something the Ghostbusters were involved with at the height of our fame. Ray decided he wanted to complete it (with the encouragement of and help from a new friend, a kid who calls himself Podcast—the first person I've ever met that was as enthusiastic about things as Ray).

I was asked to invest in a small print run of the cookbook for Ray's bookstore, and that's when I knew I had found the perfect thing to test the waters with. After all, who doesn't love a cookbook?

So, here we are, with the Ghostbusters cookbook, in all its glory. I'm a big fan of completing projects, and thanks to Ray and Podcast, you're not just getting a pile of recipes. You're getting a little piece of history.

Ghostbusters forever.

Winston Zeddemore

New York City, NY

INTRODUCTION

The culinary manual you're currently holding in your hands was originally born of a deal that Peter Venkman put together back in the '80s, a way to pay off at least one of the mortgages on my childhood home. It should've been the perfect project for a ghostwriter—but Peter wasn't always one to read a contract. The terms were clear: We had to pick the dishes we wanted in the book and write introductions for each.

Sounds simple, and it was—except for the fact that we barely had time to eat, let alone write the material needed for a book.

But we could always talk—so I came up with the idea of recording our thoughts and transcribing them later. We collected enough material en route to and from our regular caseload that we were able to get about halfway done before the whole thing was abruptly canceled—at which point all the tapes we'd recorded found a new home in a small box placed in the back corner of my storage locker in Queens, destined, most likely, to remain undiscovered until such time as the estate sale following my inevitable exit from this plane of existence.

Destiny, though, runs a crooked path . . .

Decades after what I thought was the end of professional ghostbusting, a threat rose in the heartland: the return of a Sumerian god of death, intent on realizing its goal of planetary destruction.

Gozer had traveled back to this plane of existence, and the Ghostbusters rose to the occasion, facing the beast again in the dusty front yard of a farm once owned by our recently departed colleague, Egon Spengler.

But we were not alone in our resistance: Egon's grandchildren and their friends not only identified and alerted us to the emerging threat but also joined us in putting an end to Gozer, this time for good.

What's more, I met the host of *Mystical Tales of the Unknown Universe*, a delightful young man who goes by the moniker of Podcast. During an interview for his show, this unfinished project came up, and he insisted it be completed, offering his assistance. Podcast not only found a computer program to automatically transcribe our tapes from the early '80s but also was instrumental in gathering several new recipes from the next generation of Ghostbusters, which filled out this book.

Without Podcast and his expertise in technology, food reviews, and, yes, the paranormal, the book you're reading would never have been finished.

The introductions to each recipe are direct transcriptions of either newly recorded or archival audio from 1984, making this the literary equivalent of cinema verité.

It's both a moment in time, and of the moment.

Let's eat, shall we?

—Dr. Ray Stantz

New York City, NY

PROTON PACK

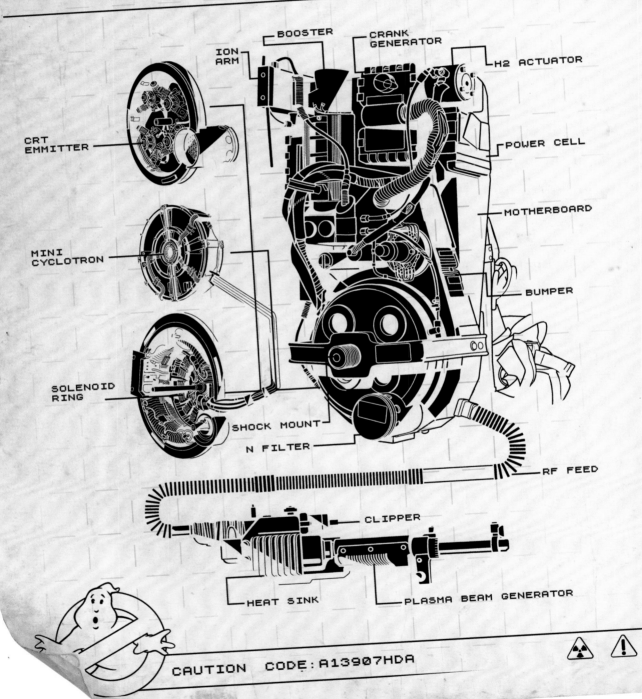

BOOSTER

CRANK GENERATOR

ION ARM

H2 ACTUATOR

CRT EMMITTER

POWER CELL

MOTHERBOARD

MINI CYCLOTRON

BUMPER

SOLENOID RING

SHOCK MOUNT

N FILTER

RF FEED

CLIPPER

HEAT SINK

PLASMA BEAM GENERATOR

CAUTION CODE: A13907HDA

KITCHEN TOOLS

BOX GRATER
Helpful for shredding foods such as cheese, or grates the skin off citrus fruits (aka zest)

COLANDER
Drains liquids through small holes

DRY MEASURING CUPS
Help you determine amounts of ingredients such as flour

FRYING PAN
Useful for cooking fried foods or for general cooking use

IMMERSION BLENDER
Turns foods into a puree

LADLE
Helpful for serving soups or stews

LIQUID MEASURING CUP
Determines exact amounts of liquids by lining up the top of a liquid to the marks on the glass

MEASURING SPOONS
Determine smaller amounts of ingredients

MINI CHOPPER
Chops small foods and ingredients like cilantro, mint, and other herbs

PROTON PACK
A necessary precaution against any ghosts that may haunt your kitchen

ROLLING PIN
Rolls out or flattens dough

RUBBER SPATULA
Helpful for folding ingredients into each other, or scraping the sides of bowls

SAUCEPAN WITH LID
Helpful for simmering or boiling foods

SPATULA
Useful for turning or flipping foods during the cooking process

STAND MIXER
Beats, whips, or mixes foods at varying speeds

WHISK
Smoothly whips or mixes liquids and batters

CHAPTER

1

ETHEREAL APPETIZERS

The practice of providing food before the meal was said to have been started by the Athenians around 206 BCE, give or take, but it's entirely possible, one might even argue likely, that they were influenced by stories of the bygone culture of Atlantis. Until hard evidence surfaces, you readers will have to make up your own minds on that. Meanwhile, here are ten fantastic hors d'oeuvre options to prime one's palate before getting down to the business of a serious meal.

PODCAST'S MARSHMALLOW FONDUE

DIFFICULTY: Easy	**YIELD:** 6 servings	**PREP TIME:** 10 Minutes	**DIETARY:** GF

PODCAST: I know we talk about marshmallows a little later in the book—shoutout to the sides section—but I want to say up front that the best way to make sure they don't come alive and start trying to ruin your life is if the marshmallow is already goo, like in this fondue recipe. Goo can't chase after you.

RAY STANTZ: I hate to say it, but if you believe that, you'll be in for a rude awakening. In my experience, it's the goo you have to be most wary of.

8 ounces mascarpone cheese

6 ounces marshmallow creme

1 cup frozen whipped topping, thawed

½ teaspoon clear vanilla extract

Fruit, for serving

1. In a medium bowl with a handheld mixer, stir together the mascarpone and marshmallow creme until just combined.

2. Fold in the whipped topping and vanilla. Refrigerate until ready to serve.

3. Serve with fruit.

EGON'S SPORES, MOLDS, AND FUNGUS STUFFED MUSHROOMS

DIFFICULTY: Medium	**YIELD:** 12 servings	**PREP TIME:** 15 minutes	**COOK TIME:** 25 minutes	**DIETARY:** V

RAY STANTZ: Egon's collection of spores, molds, and fungus was often called the envy of the free world. Sure, it might only ever have been Venkman who called it that, but the fact remains: Egon never argued the point. As he put it: "A large part of the fascination I take in my collection comes from the diversity and versatility of its components. This versatility has, on more than one occasion, allowed me to cobble together some easy sustenance during my days as an undergraduate."

While I'm usually the sucker for nostalgia, Egon was the one wandering down memory lane when he saw this recipe. As a bonus, any leftovers might make for an excellent starter set for anyone interested in following in Egon's footsteps and creating a spores, molds, and fungus collection of their own . . .

12 button mushrooms

1 tablespoon olive oil

1 tablespoon minced shallot

1 garlic clove, minced

¼ teaspoon kosher salt

¼ teaspoon ground black pepper

¼ cup seasoned bread crumbs

½ cup crumbled blue cheese

1. Remove the stems from the mushrooms. Set the caps aside and mince the stems.

2. In a large skillet over medium heat, combine the olive oil, minced stems, shallot, and garlic. Cook for 2 to 3 minutes, until softened. Season with the salt and pepper. Remove from the heat and let cool slightly.

3. Transfer the mushroom stem mixture to a large bowl. Add the bread crumbs and blue cheese, stirring to combine.

4. Preheat the oven to 375°F. Line a baking sheet with parchment paper.

5. Fill the mushroom caps with the blue cheese mixture. Arrange the stuffed mushrooms on the prepped baking sheet.

6. Bake for 15 to 20 minutes, until the mushrooms have softened and the cheese has browned. Serve warm.

DANA'S DEMON EGGS

DIFFICULTY: Medium	**YIELD:** 16 servings	**PREP TIME**: 10 minutes	**COOK TIME:** 15 minutes	**DIETARY:** GF, V

▶ ᶩᕀᶲᵢᶩᕀᶲᶩᕀᶲᶩᕀᶲᶩᕀᶲᶩᕀᶲᶩᕀᶲᶩᕀᶲ

PETER VENKMAN: So, I did a home inspection for our first client, Dana Barrett—which the lawyers want me to remind everyone is a matter of public record at this point, by the way, just in case—and I noticed a few things about her apartment. First, it had character. Charm. You don't expect the site of major haunting to have so many pastels represented in the decor. And the kitchen! That's where it all first went down—some eggs fried themselves right on the countertop. Possessed eggs? Well, they might as well be called deviled. I'd also like to add, again, thanks to my lawyers, that at no time do I recommend seeking out and/or eating possessed eggs of any kind; they can really play hell on the ol' colon, and you do not want to experience what happens when they try to come out the other side. Better to play it safe and have some actual deviled eggs, like this spicy little number we have here.

8 large eggs

3 to 4 tablespoons mayonnaise

1 teaspoon Dijon mustard

2 to 3 dashes hot sauce

¼ teaspoon ground cayenne

¼ teaspoon onion powder

¼ teaspoon kosher salt

⅛ teaspoon white pepper

¼ teaspoon paprika

2 jalapeños, sliced

1. Place the eggs into a large saucepan, covering them with 1 to 2 inches of water. Turn on the heat to medium high and bring to a boil.

2. Turn off the heat, cover with a lid, and let sit for 12 minutes. Transfer the eggs to an ice bath and let cool completely.

3. Halve the eggs. Place the yolks in a medium bowl and set aside the whites. Add the mayonnaise, mustard, hot sauce, cayenne, onion powder, salt, and white pepper to the yolks.

4. Place the mixture into a piping bag and pipe the filling into the egg white centers.

5. Sprinkle with the paprika. To serve, place a slice of jalapeño on top of each egg.

VENKMAN BURN IN HELL-APEÑO POPPERS

DIFFICULTY: Medium	**YIELD**: 24 servings	**PREP TIME**: 10 minutes	**COOK TIME**: 20 minutes	**DIETARY**: GF, V

RAY STANTZ: For all the things I love about being a Ghostbuster—and I could easily name them, sort them, rate them, and expand upon them almost endlessly with the proper amount of space, which the editors of this volume are not able to provide at this time—it's nothing like being ensconced in the world of academia. A recurring point of discussion between my colleagues and I is how different the private sector can be for those dedicated to the pursuit of scientific advancement and enlightenment by comparison . . . but one thing I noticed remained constant between academia and the real world: when Venkman rubs someone the wrong way, they're rubbed all the way wrong. Whether it's an agent of the Environmental Protection Agency or the student volunteers we regularly worked with back at the university, the words "Venkman Burn in Hell" have been heard and, in at least one case, seen more often than I or Dr. Spengler could even begin to count. These spicy jalapeño poppers are far more delightful than the infernal pit, and yet, just as likely to capture Venkman's attention, if not his immortal soul.

12 jalapeños

6 ounces cream cheese, softened

4 ounces shredded cheddar cheese

2 to 3 dashes hot sauce

½ teaspoon garlic powder

½ teaspoon onion powder

½ teaspoon kosher salt

¼ teaspoon ground black pepper

¼ cup crushed flaming hot cheese snacks

1 tablespoon unsalted butter, melted

1. Preheat the oven to 400°F. Prep a baking sheet with nonstick spray.

2. Using gloves, halve the jalapeños lengthwise. Discard the seeds and use a small spoon to scrape out the membranes. Discard membranes.

3. In a medium bowl, stir together cream cheese, cheddar cheese, hot sauce, garlic powder, onion powder, salt, and pepper. Place the mixture into a piping bag, then fill the jalapeños.

4. In a small bowl, stir together the cheese snacks and butter. Sprinkle the crumbs on top of the jalapeños.

5. Bake for 18 to 20 minutes, until the cheese has melted and the topping is crispy. Serve hot.

PETTY CASH EGG ROLLS

DIFFICULTY: Difficult	**YIELD:** 18 servings	**PREP TIME:** 20 minutes	**COOK TIME:** 20 minutes

RAY STANTZ: Every good New Yorker with a properly seasoned palate has a soft spot for the now-ubiquitous egg roll, a staple of Chinese restaurants, dive bars, and fusion chains across the five boroughs. A descendant of the spring roll, the concept of what we know of today as the egg roll was, according to accepted lore, first conceived of and executed in the Big Apple back in the 1930s. The egg roll has been a regular addition to every order I've taken out of Chinatown and has the distinction of being part of the last meal I had before my life was changed forever. The story goes that we had used the last of our initial capital to treat ourselves to a nice meal, unsure if our attempts to go into business as Ghostbusters would ever pan out. I was midchew when the alarm went off, signaling our first call, a little green terror down at the Sedgewick. Since the entire operation occurred with the taste of cabbage and pork dancing across my taste buds, that taste now reminds me of the best of times. It's good luck, and I always recommend having a roll or two before any of life's biggest moments. (Or, to be fair, whenever one is hungry for a deep-fried piece of heaven.

1 tablespoon olive oil

1 pound ground pork

1 (8-ounce) can water chestnuts, drained and minced

2 garlic cloves, minced

1 teaspoon minced fresh ginger

2 tablespoons oyster sauce

1½ tablespoons soy sauce

2 teaspoons mirin (found in the Asian aisle of a grocery)

¼ teaspoon white pepper

1 cup shredded napa cabbage

½ cup shredded carrots

2 green onions, diced

20 large egg roll wrappers

4 cups vegetable oil, for frying

½ cup sweet chili sauce, for serving

1. In a large skillet over medium heat, heat the olive oil. Add the pork, water chestnuts, garlic, and ginger and cook for 5 to 6 minutes, until the pork is cooked through and no longer pink.

2. Stir in the oyster sauce, soy sauce, mirin, and white pepper. Cook for 1 to 2 minutes, until fragrant.

3. Remove the pork mixture from the heat and transfer to a large bowl. Add the cabbage, carrots, and green onions, tossing to combine. Let the filling cool slightly.

4. Place one egg roll wrapper onto a clean surface, with a corner pointed toward you. Place ¼ cup of the pork mixture into the center and fold the corner up over the mixture. Fold the left and right corners toward the center and roll up. Add a dab of water onto the corner to seal. Repeat with the remaining egg roll wrappers and filling.

5. In a Dutch oven, heat the vegetable oil to 375°F. Working in batches as needed to prevent crowding, fry the egg rolls for 4 to 5 minutes, until browned. Drain on a wire rack.

6. Serve with the sweet chili sauce.

LOUIS'S PARTY BRIE

DIFFICULTY: Easy	**YIELD**: 8 servings	**PREP TIME**: 10 minutes	**COOK TIME**: 15 Minutes	**DIETARY**: GF, V

RAY STANTZ: Popular since at least the eighth century, when the emperor Charlemagne developed a taste for it, Brie is, like champagne, only considered worthy of the name when produced in a specific way and in a specific location. That location being France. I don't know that I subscribe to such a rigid definition, but if there's one thing I learned, it doesn't pay to get into a discussion of semantics with a food snob of any stripe. Brie was, and I suspect remains, one of the musts for any party hosted by our extant accountant, Louis Tully. When the line for the smoked salmon is impenetrable, you head for the Brie.

PODCAST: For anyone who still doesn't know what Brie is, it's basically like if nacho cheese had a super-fancy cousin that only watched movies nobody heard of and said they did all the cool stuff before it was popular—but it tastes better with crackers.

8 ounces Brie

½ cup honey

1 tablespoon balsamic vinegar

½ cup dried cranberries

½ cup pecans, chopped

1 tablespoon dried rosemary leaves

1 teaspoon grated lemon zest

Crackers, for serving

1. Preheat the oven to 350°F. Line a baking sheet with parchment paper.

2. Place the Brie on the prepped baking sheet. Bake for 15 minutes, until softened.

3. Meanwhile, in a small saucepan, combine the honey, balsamic vinegar, cranberries, and pecans. Bring to a boil, then remove from the heat.

4. Move the Brie to a serving plate. Pour the honey mixture over it. Sprinkle with the rosemary and lemon zest.

5. Serve with crackers.

EGON, YOUR GUACAMOLE

DIFFICULTY: Easy	**YIELD:** 8 servings	**PREP TIME:** 10 minutes	**DIETARY:** GF, V, V+

PETER VENKMAN: When it comes to doing science, Egon always likes to say that "the most important thing is to collect as much data as you can." And I can get behind that, y'know, in a general sense. Thing is, the data Egon usually likes to collect is moist, smelly, sticky, and sometimes it moves—kinda like the floor of the men's room at Grand Central Station. Gross stuff. That's bad enough, but he goes out of his way to ask me to collect it for him! I'm starting to think he finds it funny. What was I talking about? Oh, right—guacamole. Folks, this stuff is a must-have at any holiday party, game night, or ghostly gathering. It's tangy, it's fresh, it's practically a salad. The only thing that's bad about this stuff is the color—gives me flashbacks to something I scraped up for Egon once.

2 avocados, pitted and peeled

1 small shallot, minced

1 garlic clove, minced

2 teaspoons lime juice

2 to 3 dashes hot sauce

½ teaspoon kosher salt

¼ teaspoon ground black pepper

¼ teaspoon ground cayenne

1 small jalapeño, diced

2 tablespoons chopped fresh cilantro

Tortilla chips, for serving

1. In a medium bowl, lightly mash the avocados.

2. Stir in the shallot, garlic, lime juice, hot sauce, salt, pepper, and cayenne.

3. Fold in the jalapeño and cilantro.

4. Cover with plastic wrap, pressing to the surface of the guacamole to prevent browning. Refrigerate until ready to serve.

5. Serve with tortilla chips.

FARMHOUSE FRENCH ONION SOUP

| **DIFFICULTY:** Medium | **YIELD:** 4 servings | **PREP TIME:** 20 minutes | **COOK TIME:** 1 hour |

PODCAST: Okay, so I was over at Phoebe's house, and I saw all these bowls in the sink and I'm, like, "those look weird," and Phoebe just stared at me like I didn't know something obvious. Then her mom comes in and says, "Those are supposed to be for French onion soup," and I'm all, "I just use regular cereal bowls for soup." Phoebe sighed, adjusted her glasses, and gave me a look that screamed exasperation. And then she said, "French onion soup bowls are oven safe, because that's where you finish the soup. Because they withstand heat up to 1000°C—hotter than a typical home oven can reach. I also use these bowls for occasional experiments. Don't ever eat out of the one with an X on the bottom."

So, I learned something! Technically two things, but only one of those things is going to apply to you. Still, whatever kind of bowl it comes in, French onion soup is a great comfort food (at least, that's what I've heard old people say), and now you can make it yourself!

---

6 tablespoons unsalted butter

4 large onions, sliced

½ teaspoon kosher salt

4 cups beef broth

½ cup red wine

1 tablespoon Worcestershire sauce

2 sprigs fresh thyme

1 bay leaf

¼ teaspoon ground black pepper

4 large slices baguette, toasted

1 cup shredded Gruyère cheese

1. In a Dutch oven over medium-high heat, combine the butter, onions, and salt. Cook for 30 minutes, until the onions are caramelized.

2. Pour in the beef broth, red wine, and Worcestershire sauce. Add the thyme and bay leaf. Reduce the heat to medium low and simmer for 20 minutes.

3. Remove and discard the thyme and bay leaf. Stir in the pepper.

4. Preheat the oven broiler. Arrange the bread slices on a baking sheet and broil for 3 minutes, turning once, until well toasted on both sides. Remove from the heat; do not turn off broiler.

5. Place four oven-safe crocks onto a baking sheet. Ladle the soup into the bowls, then top each one with a slice of toasted bread and then the Gruyère cheese.

6. Broil for 3 to 4 minutes, until the cheese is golden brown. Serve immediately.

INTERDIMENSIONAL CROSS-RIP DIP

| **DIFFICULTY**: Easy | **YIELD:** 12 servings | **PREP TIME**: 10 minutes | **DIETARY**: GF, V |

PODCAST: It's been fun coming up with names and stuff for some of these recipes, and I have the perfect name for the ten-layer dip: the interdimensional cross-rip dip!

RAY STANTZ: Is it because of the long history of interdimensional cross-rips across the ages? Northern Niger at the center of the Sahara? Tunguska, site of the 1909 blast? Maybe either of Gozer's attempted incursions upon this dimensional plane?

PODCAST: Actually, I just thought it was cool that *cross-rip* and *dip* rhyme.

RAY STANTZ: Sometimes it's best not to overthink these things. That said, now that you mention it, the ten layers of the dip do remind me of photos of the aftermath from Tunguska and the blast patterns from the waves of spectral force that flattened the earth for thousands of square miles in every direction. Either way, now I've got a hankering for some tortilla chips.

1 (16-ounce) can refried beans

1 tablespoon chili powder

½ teaspoon ground cumin

½ teaspoon garlic powder

½ teaspoon paprika

½ teaspoon kosher salt

¼ teaspoon onion powder

¼ teaspoon ground black pepper

2 cups Egon, Your Guacamole (page 27) or store-bought

2 cups salsa

2 cups shredded iceberg lettuce

2 cups shredded cheddar cheese

1 large tomato, diced

1 cup sour cream

2 green onions, diced

1 (2.25-ounce) can sliced olives, drained

½ cup crumbled queso fresco

Tortilla chips, for serving

1. In a medium bowl, stir together the refried beans, chili powder, cumin, garlic powder, paprika, salt, onion powder, and pepper. Spread the bean mixture across the bottom of a 9-by-13-inch baking pan.

2. Spread the guacamole on top of the beans, then spread on the salsa.

3. Add the lettuce, then sprinkle over the cheese, then the tomato.

4. Drizzle on the sour cream.

5. Sprinkle on the green onions, then the olives, and finish with the queso fresco.

6. Cover with plastic wrap and refrigerate until ready to serve.

7. Serve with chips.

SHANDOR MINING COMPANY PULL-APART BREAD

DIFFICULTY: Difficult	**YIELD**: 10 servings	**PREP TIME**: 3 hours 30 minutes	**COOK TIME**: 30 minutes	**DIETARY**: V

PODCAST: Summerville grew out of the Shandor mine. We're a mining town. I'm not exactly sure what the local economy has been based on ever since, but I'm twelve. I don't think about those kinds of things.

RAY STANTZ: Well, sometimes towns are just stubborn enough to stick around long past the time that their original motor of commerce has sputtered and died. And other times, well, they become ghost towns.

PODCAST: That was the worst pun I've ever heard! And I love it. Anyway, one of the things the miners did leave behind here in Summerville was a huge love of bread. Spinners Roller Hop has a whole section in their menu about it. They couldn't get enough. I don't know that they ever went with garlic Parmesan, but that's what this recipe is, so we're gonna roll with it. (Get it? A little bread pun—did it get a rise out of anyone?)

DOUGH

¾ cup warm milk (110°F)

1 envelope (2¼ teaspoons) dry yeast

2¼ cups all-purpose flour

1 tablespoon honey

1 teaspoon kosher salt

1 large egg

1 tablespoon olive oil, for greasing

SPREAD

8 tablespoons (1 stick) unsalted butter, softened

2 garlic cloves, minced

¼ cup grated Parmesan cheese

½ teaspoon dried basil, crushed

½ teaspoon dried oregano, crushed

½ teaspoon kosher salt

TO MAKE THE DOUGH:

1. In the bowl of an electric stand mixer fitted with the dough hook, sprinkle the yeast over the warm milk and let sit for 5 minutes, until foamy.

2. Add the flour, honey, salt, and egg, then knead for 5 minutes, until the dough is smooth and elastic. Grease a large bowl with the olive oil. Transfer the dough to the prepped bowl, turning to coat. Cover with plastic wrap and let rise for 2 hours, until doubled in size.

TO MAKE THE SPREAD:

1. In a small bowl, stir together the butter, garlic, Parmesan cheese, basil, oregano, and salt. Set aside.

2. Punch down the dough, then turn it out onto a lightly floured surface. Cut the dough into ten equal pieces. Grease a loaf pan with the olive oil.

3. Pat out the dough pieces into 4-inch squares. Spread the butter mixture onto one side of a square. Fold in half, then place in the prepped loaf pan. Repeat with the remaining dough squares, spreading the remaining butter on top of the loaf.

4. Cover the pan with plastic wrap, refrigerate, and let dough rise for 1 hour.

5. Preheat the oven to 350°F.

6. Discard the plastic wrap and bake for 25 to 30 minutes, until golden brown. Serve warm.

CHAPTER

(2)

MANIFESTING THE MAINS

Fun fact: In the United States and most of Canada, the word *entrée* is synonymous with "main course." But the Québécois and many nations operate differently, citing the entrée as an element of the meal served before the main course. Language evolves, and the meanings of words can change. It's important to take note of these things when you can, so you can spare yourself a little disaster if you're ever forced to interact or communicate with a spectral presence that you're trying to keep calm. Always understand the words you use as best you can! That advice given, we can now move on to these ten fantastic dishes, any one of which could form the centerpiece to your evening meal.

FIREHOUSE CHILI ON THE GO

| **DIFFICULTY:** Medium | **YIELD:** 8 servings | **PREP TIME:** 20 minutes | **COOK TIME:** 1 hour 10 minutes | **DIETARY:** GF |

WINSTON ZEDDEMORE: First thing I learned when I got this job, man, is that it is go, go, go. I've never been so busy in my life—which doesn't leave a lot of time to get a good meal in, you know? And you gotta keep your strength up. Packs are heavy, there's a lot of running. It's a real workout. Egon and Ray can get by with eating like they are still college kids, but I gotta have something more substantial—and I finally found my go-to with this recipe. Buddy of mine used to call these feedbags, right? Portable hot chow you can eat on the run. Now, some people prefer salads or even walking tacos, but in my opinion, you just can't beat chili. Could be nostalgia, since we work out of a firehouse, and firemen have such a connection to this stuff—but it's just straight-up satisfying. (Bonus, it's easy to make a big batch of, so friends, family, and colleagues can each have some of their own.)

2 tablespoons olive oil

1 large onion, diced

1 green bell pepper, diced

2 ribs celery, diced

2 garlic cloves, minced

1 pound ground beef

1 (28-ounce) can diced tomatoes

1 (14-ounce) can tomato sauce

1 (14.5-ounce) can kidney beans, drained

1 tablespoon tomato paste

1 tablespoon Worcestershire sauce

2 tablespoons chili powder

1 tablespoon packed light brown sugar

1 teaspoon dried basil

1 teaspoon ground cumin

1 teaspoon paprika

½ teaspoon kosher salt

¼ teaspoon ground black pepper

¼ teaspoon ground cayenne

1 bay leaf

8 (1-ounce) bags corn chips

1 cup shredded cheddar cheese

1 cup sour cream

2 green onions, diced

1. In a Dutch oven over medium-high heat, heat the olive oil. Add the onion, bell pepper, celery, and garlic and cook for 3 to 4 minutes, until softened.

2. Add the ground beef and cook for 5 to 6 minutes, until browned and no longer pink.

3. Stir in the tomatoes, tomato sauce, kidney beans, tomato paste, and Worcestershire sauce.

4. Add the chili powder, brown sugar, basil, cumin, paprika, salt, pepper, cayenne, and bay leaf. Bring to a boil, then reduce the heat to low, cover, and simmer for 1 hour.

5. To serve, open a bag of chips and add a large spoonful of the chili. Top with the cheddar cheese, sour cream, and green onions. Repeat with the remaining chips and chili.

TERROR DOGS

DIFFICULTY: Medium	**YIELD:** 8 servings	**PREP TIME:** 4 hours 10 minutes	**COOK TIME:** 10 minutes

PODCAST: Okay, those things that possessed Mr. Grooberson, Phoebe's mom, Callie, and Lucky—they were called Terror Dogs? On what planet would anyone think those were dogs?

RAY STANTZ: That's the question, isn't it? The Gatekeeper, Zuul, and the Keymaster, Vinz Clortho—minions of Gozer and the device by which the genocidal god makes its way from dimension to dimension—take for their corporeal form when interacting with the physical plane two muscular horned quadrupeds that look more like the unholy spawn of an ox and a shaved bear than any canine I've ever come across. But they do like to wag their tails and are quite affectionate toward their master, giving them the energetic demeanor of a pooch, if nothing else, and may well be equivalent to a dog in some remote corner of the multiverse. Anyway, "Terror Dogs" seemed like as good a descriptor as any when we sat down to write it all up.

PODCAST: I'm just gonna pretend you said, like, Mars. Anyway, the name makes me think of an evil hot dog. And what would an evil hot dog be? Like, a wiener covered with a bunch of spicy toppings and barbecue stuff? Beware the peppers of my terror dog!

RAY STANTZ: No, son. An evil hot dog would be a sausage possessed by the devil himself. Barbecue toppings are more my idea of the trimmings on a heavenly frank.

COLESLAW

½ cup mayonnaise

2 tablespoons granulated sugar

1 tablespoon apple cider vinegar

½ teaspoon celery seed

¼ teaspoon kosher salt

¼ teaspoon ground black pepper

3 cups shredded green cabbage

1 cup shredded red cabbage

1 cup shredded carrots

HOT DOGS

8 hot dog buns

8 hot dogs

2 cups crushed potato chips

½ cup barbecue sauce

½ cup crema

½ cup sliced jalapeño

TO MAKE THE COLESLAW:

1. In a medium bowl, stir together the mayonnaise, sugar, apple cider vinegar, celery seed, salt, and pepper. In a large bowl, combine the green cabbage, red cabbage, and carrots. Add the dressing and toss to combine. Cover and refrigerate for 4 hours.

TO MAKE THE HOT DOGS:

1. Toast the hot dog buns.

2. In a large skillet over medium heat, cook the hot dogs until warmed through, about 10 minutes. Place them in the toasted buns.

3. To serve, top with coleslaw and the crushed potato chips. Drizzle over the barbecue sauce and crema, then top with the jalapeños.

JANINE'S WORLD'S FAIR FALAFEL

DIFFICULTY: Medium	**YIELD:** 4 servings	**PREP TIME:** 15 minutes	**COOK TIME:** 5 minutes	**DIETARY:** V, V+

JANINE MELNITZ: I've lived in New York all my life, and I've seen so many things—wonderful things, terrible things—and that was just on the subway. Working for the Ghostbusters, I got to see a whole new side of this city, and it was scary. When the mayor sent Dr. Spengler and the others over to Central Park West, there was just something in the air—everyone could feel it—and I thought that the world really might come to an end. Funny thing is, I didn't mope. I got nostalgic for the good times, like going to the world's fair when I was little. There was a man in a jet pack, I think, and we had falafel, which was fabulous . . . until we found out my mother was allergic to chickpeas. But even that didn't spoil our time. I got a nice souvenir coin from the fair, and it always brought me a little luck—and I'll tell you, I gave that coin to Egon right before he saved the world. I guess you could say I had a small part in it. And I am really craving falafel right now . . .

1 (15-ounce) can chickpeas, drained and rinsed

2 garlic cloves, minced

½ cup minced onion

¼ cup minced fresh parsley

3 tablespoons cornstarch

1 tablespoon ground coriander

1 tablespoon ground cumin

½ teaspoon kosher salt

¼ teaspoon ground black pepper

2 cups vegetable oil, for frying

Hummus, for serving

Pita, for serving

1. In a food processor, combine the chickpeas, garlic, onion, parsley, cornstarch, coriander, cumin, salt, and pepper. Pulse until smooth.

2. Form the mixture into 2-inch round balls.

3. In a large, deep skillet, heat the vegetable oil over medium-high heat to 350°F. Add the falafel and fry for 3 to 4 minutes, until browned. Let drain on a wire rack.

4. Serve with hummus and pita.

THREE MORTGAGE SOUP

DIFFICULTY: Medium	**YIELD:** 6 servings	**PREP TIME:** 10 minutes	**COOK TIME:** 1 hour 50 minutes	**DIETARY:** GF

RAY STANTZ: Most people don't know this, but the initial round of investment capital required to open the doors of Ghostbusters Inc. came from me, in the form of a third mortgage that I took out on my family home. I was born in that house. I grew up in that house. And, on cold winter evenings, my sainted mother would slip into that house's grand old kitchen and fix me up a hot bowl of soup with whatever she happened to have on hand. Soup is like a warm hug in a bowl, the kind of comfort and reassurance that's nice to have whether you're at one of life's many crossroads, you've fallen prey to some insidious germ, or the temperature has just dropped to a cozy 50°F. This recipe will fit the bill for any situation where a hearty soup is required, and then some!

2 pounds boneless chuck roast, cubed

2 teaspoons kosher salt

½ teaspoon ground black pepper

2 tablespoons olive oil

8 cups water

1 pound creamer potatoes, halved

2 large carrots, peeled and cut into 2-inch chunks

1 zucchini, cut into 2-inch chunks

1 cup halved fresh green beans

2 ears corn, cut into thirds

1 small cabbage, cut into wedges

2 cups salsa, for serving

1. Season the beef with the salt and pepper.

2. In a large Dutch oven over medium heat, heat the olive oil. Add the beef and brown on all sides, about 5 minutes total.

3. Add the water and bring to a boil. Lower heat to low, cover, and simmer for 1 hour.

4. Add the potatoes, carrots, zucchini, and beans. Cover and simmer for 30 minutes.

5. Add in the corn and cabbage, cover, and simmer for another 15 minutes.

6. Serve in bowls, topped with salsa.

KUNG PAO SHRIMP

DIFFICULTY: Medium	**YIELD:** 6 servings	**PREP TIME:** 10 minutes	**COOK TIME:** 10 minutes

PODCAST: We're talking to Summerville teacher Gary Grooberson, who not only shows the best movies in class but also was once possessed by a Terror Dog named Vinz Clortho. But his main expertise is in local restaurants.

GARY GROOBERSON: Actually, it's seismology?

PODCAST: This is called setting the mood. Just go with it. Tell me about a meal you'd recommend to the readers of a cookbook.

GARY GROOBERSON: Okay! Okay. Well, I kind of like to go with kung pao shrimp. It's always nice to get a little seafood when you live so far from the ocean, and Chinese food usually feels like it's on the healthy side of things, especially when it's the spicier kind. Although if someone had a shellfish allergy—maybe I should change my answer?

PODCAST Uh, I think I'm going to ask Phoebe's mom now.

GARY GROOBERSON: That's fair.

SAUCE

1 tablespoon water

1 teaspoon cornstarch

3 tablespoons soy sauce

1 tablespoon rice vinegar

1 teaspoon sesame oil

1 teaspoon packed light brown sugar

SHRIMP

1 pound raw shrimp, peeled and cleaned

1 tablespoon soy sauce

2 teaspoons cornstarch

⅛ teaspoon white pepper

STIR-FRY

1 tablespoon vegetable oil

2 garlic cloves, minced

1 teaspoon minced fresh ginger

6 small dried chiles

1 small onion, quartered

1 red bell pepper, diced

¼ cup cashews

1 green onion, minced

TO MAKE THE SAUCE:

1. In a medium bowl, stir together the water and cornstarch until combined. Whisk in the soy sauce, rice vinegar, sesame oil, and brown sugar. Set aside.

TO MAKE THE SHRIMP:

1. In a large bowl, toss the shrimp with the soy sauce, cornstarch, and white pepper. Set aside.

TO MAKE THE STIR-FRY:

1. In a wok or large skillet over medium-high heat, heat the vegetable oil. Add the garlic and ginger and cook for 1 to 2 minutes, until fragrant. Add the chiles, onion, bell pepper, and cashews and cook for 3 to 4 minutes, until the vegetables have softened.

2. Add the shrimp and cook for 3 to 4 minutes, until no longer pink.

3. Pour in the sauce and toss to coat. Cook for 1 minute, until the sauce has thickened.

4. Sprinkle with the green onion, then serve.

SPINNERS' SEISMIC BURGER

DIFFICULTY: Medium	**YIELD:** 1 to 3 servings	**PREP TIME:** 15 minutes	**COOK TIME:** 10 minutes

RAY STANTZ: After dealing with the unexpected reemergence of Gozer the Gozerian in the heart of Middle America, I'll admit I worked up a powerful hunger. Thankfully, the smaller towns of flyover country come equipped with some of the best mom-and-pop restaurants outside of Manhattan. My personal favorite was Spinners, a traditional 1950s-style burger joint that I immediately fell in love with—from the crispy, crinkle-cut French fries cooked in real tallow to the heavenly, borderline-mystical aroma of burgers that are only ever this good in the heart of cattle country.

The best burger I had at Spinners was created in honor of the unusual seismic activity that troubled the town, caused by the countermeasures Egon Spengler set up to slow Gozer's return. The burger was meant to be so big that it shook the earth. And let me say, it was so good that I made a special point, when it came to completing this cookbook, to request a recreation be included. You can thank me later, and what's more, you'll want to.

Spinners Roller Hop

SAUCE

2 tablespoons mayonnaise

2 teaspoons ketchup

2 teaspoons relish

¼ teaspoon packed light brown sugar

⅛ teaspoon white pepper

PATTIES

1½ pounds ground beef

1 garlic clove, minced

1 tablespoon Worcestershire sauce

1 teaspoon dried basil

1 teaspoon onion powder

½ teaspoon paprika

½ teaspoon kosher salt

½ teaspoon ground black pepper

2 slices cheddar cheese

2 slices Swiss cheese

BURGER

1 hamburger bun

2 slices red onion

2 slices tomato

2 iceberg lettuce leaves

1 gherkin pickle

ADDITIONAL SUPPLIES

1 (4-inch) skewer

TO MAKE THE SAUCE:

1. In a small bowl, stir together the mayonnaise, ketchup, relish, brown sugar, and white pepper. Refrigerate until ready to use.

TO MAKE THE PATTIES:

1. In a large bowl, mix together the ground beef, garlic, Worcestershire sauce, basil, onion powder, paprika, salt, and pepper, until just combined. Form into four equal flattened patties, ½-inch thick.

2. On a grill pan over medium-high heat, cook the patties for 3 to 4 minutes on one side, until browned. Flip them over. Add one slice of either cheddar or Swiss cheese to each patty. Cook for another 2 to 3 minutes, until medium or desired doneness is reached and the cheese is melted.

TO MAKE THE BURGERS:

1. Place the bottom bun on a serving plate. Add a cheddar cheese patty, followed by a Swiss cheese patty, the remaining cheddar cheese patty, and finally the remaining Swiss cheese patty.

2. Add the sauce, then the onion, tomato, and lettuce. Use the skewer to secure the burger with the gherkin on top. Serve right away, cutting into thirds if you plan to share.

CALLIE'S QUESADILLAS

DIFFICULTY: Easy	**YIELD:** 4 servings	**PREP TIME:** 10 minutes	**COOK TIME:** 30 minutes

PODCAST: So, you know I'm working on a book with Dr. Stantz.

CALLIE SPENGLER: About ghosts? You know, I don't know very much about them.

PODCAST: Your dad was Egon Spengler. You were possessed by Zuul. How can you not know anything about ghosts?

CALLIE SPENGLER: When you kids grow up, you're going to learn about repression. It's a great part of adulthood.

PODCAST: Okay. Um, actually, we're finishing a cookbook? I was going to ask about your go-to meal.

CALLIE SPENGLER: Okay, well, ah, quesadillas. I always go with quesadillas. There are, uh, carbs, and protein, and—look, it's melted cheese. No one has ever gone wrong with melted cheese. It's un-screw-uppable. Kids love it. For a mom, a quick and easy meal that kids love is the holy grail. All hail the quesadilla.

1 tablespoon olive oil

½ cup diced red onion

1 cup drained black beans

1 cup corn

1 ½ cups shredded cooked rotisserie chicken

1 teaspoon chili powder

½ teaspoon ground cumin

½ teaspoon garlic powder

¼ teaspoon onion powder

¼ teaspoon paprika

¼ teaspoon kosher salt

¼ teaspoon ground black pepper

8 slices pepper Jack cheese

2 cup shredded Monterey Jack cheese

8 flour tortillas

½ cup Egon, Your Guacamole (page 27) or store-bought

½ cup salsa

½ cup sour cream

1. In a large skillet over medium heat, heat the olive oil. Add the onion and cook for 2 to 3 minutes, until softened.

2. Add the black beans, corn, chicken, chili powder, cumin, garlic powder, onion powder, paprika, salt, and pepper. Cook for 2 to 3 minutes, until warmed through. Set aside.

3. In a medium skillet over medium heat, place one tortilla. Add two slices of pepper Jack cheese. Top with a fourth of the chicken mixture, then ½ cup of the Monterey Jack cheese. Top with a second tortilla. Cook for 2 to 3 minutes, until the cheese is melted. Flip the quesadilla over and cook for another 2 to 3 minutes, until lightly browned.

4. Remove the quesadilla from skillet and cut into quarters. Repeat with the remaining tortillas and filling.

5. Serve with the guacamole, salsa, and sour cream.

PHOEBE'S PIZZA PUZZLE

DIFFICULTY: Medium	**YIELD:** 4 servings	**PREP TIME:** 1 minute	**COOK TIME:** 15 minutes	**DIETARY:** V

PHOEBE SPENGLER: My mom is correct about melted cheese. It can't really be messed up. That reminds me, I know a joke about cheese. Do you know what kind is a cannibal's favorite? 'Orgonzola!

I shared that joke with you because I don't really have a favorite recipe, but Podcast and Dr. Stantz still wanted to include me in the completed edition of this book. I will add that I do think it's fun to cut pizza into geometric shapes beyond just squares and triangles, though. It's very satisfying. I think everyone should try it.

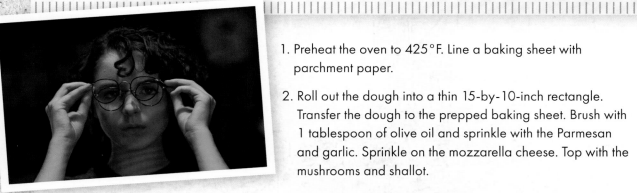

1. Preheat the oven to 425°F. Line a baking sheet with parchment paper.

2. Roll out the dough into a thin 15-by-10-inch rectangle. Transfer the dough to the prepped baking sheet. Brush with 1 tablespoon of olive oil and sprinkle with the Parmesan and garlic. Sprinkle on the mozzarella cheese. Top with the mushrooms and shallot.

3. In a small bowl, stir together the ricotta, lemon zest, salt, and pepper. Drop large dollops on top of the pizza.

4. Bake for 15 minutes, until the crust is browned.

5. Drizzle on the remaining 1 tablespoon of olive oil. Top with the basil.

6. To serve, cut into odd-size puzzle-pieces.

Store-bought pizza dough

2 tablespoons olive oil, divided

1 tablespoon grated Parmesan cheese

1 garlic clove, minced

1½ cups shredded mozzarella cheese

1 cup sliced cremini mushrooms

1 shallot, thinly sliced

1 cup ricotta cheese

1 teaspoon grated lemon zest

¼ teaspoon kosher salt

¼ teaspoon ground black pepper

6 to 8 fresh basil leaves, torn

TREVOR'S GREASE BOMB PATTY MELT

| **DIFFICULTY:** Medium | **YIELD:** 4 servings | **PREP TIME:** 15 minutes | **COOK TIME:** 50 minutes |

PODCAST: We're talking with Trevor Spengler, and I think the question that will be on everyone's mind is: Is your whole family, like, totally obsessed with cheese? I mean, your mom loves quesadillas. Phoebe has cheese puns for days. And Ray said your grandpa Egon inhaled those little cheese crackers by the pound. Sounds like obsession to me.

TREVOR SPENGLER: What? No. Why would you—no!

PODCAST: So, if I asked you for your favorite food, you wouldn't say something with cheese? What is your favorite food?

TREVOR SPENGLER: Patty melt. Wait—

PODCAST: So. Taste preferences. Are they a genetic thing, or could they be something more sinister? Oh man, that'd make a great episode of the show . . .

TREVOR SPENGLER: You're a weird kid, you know that?

ONIONS

2 tablespoons unsalted butter

1 large onion, sliced

PATTY MELT

1½ pounds ground beef

1 tablespoon Worcestershire sauce

1 teaspoon garlic powder

1 teaspoon onion powder

1 teaspoon paprika

½ teaspoon kosher salt

½ teaspoon ground black pepper

1 tablespoon vegetable oil

4 tablespoons unsalted butter, softened

8 slices sourdough bread

8 slices Swiss cheese

TO MAKE THE ONIONS:

1. In a medium skillet over medium heat, melt the butter. Add the onion and cook for about 20 minutes, until the onion is browned and caramelized. Set aside.

TO MAKE THE PATTY MELT:

1. In a large bowl, combine the ground beef, Worcestershire sauce, garlic powder, onion powder, paprika, salt, and pepper. Divide and form the mixture into four equal patties.

2. In a large skillet over medium heat, warm the vegetable oil. Add the patties and cook for 4 minutes on each side, or until cooked to medium. Remove the patties from the pan and set aside. Wipe out the skillet with a paper towel.

3. Spread the butter onto one side of each slice of bread.

4. In the same large skillet over medium heat, place one slice, buttered side down. Top with one slice of cheese, a patty, a quarter of the caramelized onions, a second slice of cheese, and another slice of bread, buttered side up. Cook for 2 to 3 minutes on each side, until golden brown and the cheese has melted. Repeat with the remaining ingredients.

5. To serve, halve the patty melts.

SUMMERVILLE (RUST CITY) CHICKEN FRIED STEAK

DIFFICULTY: Medium	**YIELD:** 4 servings	**PREP TIME:** 25 minutes	**COOK TIME:** 40 minutes

PODCAST: A good interviewer always holds on to his opinion until the end, right? My favorite meal, and the one I asked for, is chicken fried steak. I can't believe no one else said it! (Well, maybe Phoebe's family, but they're from out of town.)

When I was a kid, I thought people were ordering chicken steaks and that they were, like, really big chicken nuggets. When I finally had one it was—wow. I get it. It's steak that's fried like chicken, not a steak made from chicken. You probably knew that. Or maybe you didn't.

Is this the reason we don't call big slabs of chicken chicken steak? Anyone know? Hit me up—we can do a segment on MTUU about it.

STEAK

1½ pounds cube steaks, cut into 4 pieces

¾ cup all-purpose flour

1 teaspoon paprika

1 teaspoon kosher salt

1 teaspoon ground black pepper

½ teaspoon baking powder

½ teaspoon garlic powder

½ teaspoon onion powder

¾ cups buttermilk

1 large egg

1 to 2 dashes hot sauce

1 cup vegetable oil, for frying

GRAVY

4 tablespoons unsalted butter

¼ cup all-purpose flour

2 cups whole milk

1 teaspoon kosher salt

½ teaspoon ground black pepper

TO MAKE THE STEAK:

1. In a shallow dish, whisk together the flour, paprika, salt, pepper, baking powder, garlic powder, and onion powder. Set aside.

2. In a second shallow dish, whisk together the buttermilk, egg, and hot sauce. Set aside.

3. In a large skillet over medium-high heat, heat the vegetable oil to 350°F.

4. Dredge the steaks in the flour mixture, then the egg mixture. Dredge them in the flour a second time, shaking off the excess.

5. Working in batches, add the steaks to the oil and fry for 3 to 4 minutes on each side, until golden brown. Let drain on a wire rack.

TO MAKE THE GRAVY:

1. Remove most of the grease from the skillet. Turn the heat to medium, add the butter and flour, and cook until thickened and slightly browned, about 2 minutes. Whisk in the milk and cook for 8 to 10 minutes, until smooth. Season with the salt and pepper.

2. To serve, pour gravy over the steaks.

CHAPTER

3

SPECTRAL SIDES

Side dishes are like the lizard people of the dinner table— they can be anything they want to be. They can be vegetables. They can be a brick of mac and cheese. They can be a scoop of whipped cream and fruit. All they need to do is be to the side of the main course. The possibilities, like the nameless horrors that lurk undetected in the night, are endless.

HOW TO MAKE AN EDIBLE MINI-PUFT

| **DIFFICULTY:** Easy | **YIELD:** 1 servings | **PREP TIME**: 10 minutes | **DIETARY:** GF |

PODCAST: I feel like this chapter is going to give me nightmares. I saw the list. I know there are marshmallows involved, like, right away. Do you know how hard it is to get marshmallow goo out of your hair when it gets hard? I had to shave my head! I had to become a hat guy! I'm not a hat guy!

RAY STANTZ: Son, you were covered in the remains of a handful of gremlin-size marshmallow avatars. I witnessed the destruction of a Mr. Stay Puft that stood a hundred feet tall if he was an inch, and when he exploded, his gooey mass covered two and a half city blocks and at least 20 percent of Central Park. I was scrubbing for a month and a half.

PODCAST: But did you have to shave your head?

RAY STANTZ: Not with the chemicals commonly found in shampoo at the time. Still, the marshmallow man is not only a key component to the legend of the Ghostbusters—marshmallow as an ingredient is an accessory to a trove of tasty treats that we'd be foolish to exclude. Besides, you can feel like you're taking revenge when you whip up and destroy one of the cute little decorative marshmallow men, as seen here, and they can't do a thing to stop you.*

PODCAST: You hope.

HEAD

1 regular marshmallow

1 mini marshmallow

1 piece blue taffy

1 small piece red fondant

BODY

1 giant marshmallow

2 mini marshmallows

ADDITIONAL SUPPLIES

edible-ink pen

TO MAKE THE HEAD:

1. Cut a third of the regular marshmallow away (crosswise) and discard it. On the remaining part of the marshmallow, use the edible-ink pen to create the face details.

2. Roll out the mini marshmallow until flat. Set aside. Roll out the blue taffy and use a ¾-inch round cutter to cut out a circle. Press onto the flattened mini marshmallow and place onto the head to create the hat. Cut a ½-inch strip of red fondant and place on top of the hat for the tassel. Set aside.

TO MAKE THE BODY:

1. Cut the giant marshmallow in half crosswise and place it, sticky side down, onto a small piece of parchment paper.

2. For the hands, cut one mini marshmallow in half crosswise. Onto each half, make 2 to 3 small cuts to create the fingers. Press onto the upper half of the body to create the hands.

3. For the feet, cut the remaining mini marshmallow in half crosswise and press both onto the lower half of the body to create the feet.

4. To serve, press the head onto the body.

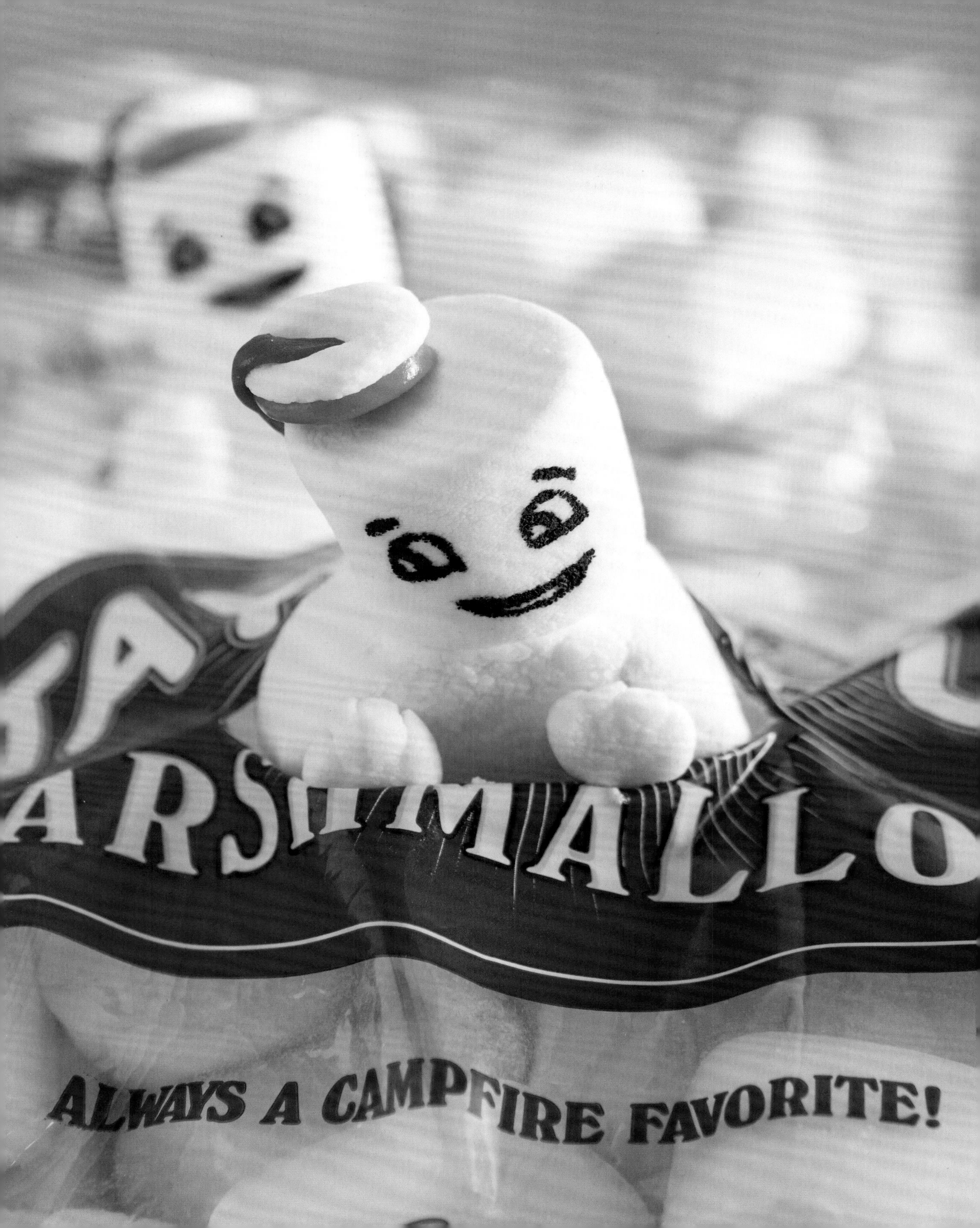
ALWAYS A CAMPFIRE FAVORITE!

GHOSTBUSTIN' SWEET POTATOES

DIFFICULTY: Medium	**YIELD:** 8 servings	**PREP TIME:** 30 minutes	**COOK TIME:** 40 minutes	**DIETARY:** GF

RAY STANTZ: In the summer of 1917, three Portuguese shepherds, children all, claimed that they were visited by a spectral apparition that told them there would be a miraculous occurrence near the city of Fatima on October 13 of that year. On the day, a rainstorm ended and the clouds forcibly parted, revealing the sun to the crowds of people who had come after hearing word of the impending miracle. The sun was pale, and able to be looked upon without hurting one's eyes. It danced in the sky and dried the drenched clothes of the onlookers—and then it was over. Fully unexplained, it was deemed the Miracle of the Sun, or el Milagre del Sol, and it remains a high point in the paranormal history of Earth.

In the United States, during the very same time, a recipe was circulated recommending the addition of marshmallow to sweet potatoes. This mix of sweet and savory caught on and became a longstanding tradition at Thanksgiving meals across the country. Which is a miracle in and of itself.

Whether or not that's as life-altering a happening as el Milagre del Sol is completely up to you.

3 large sweet potatoes, peeled and cubed

¼ cup heavy cream

4 tablespoons unsalted butter, softened

½ cup packed light brown sugar

2 tablespoons maple syrup

1 teaspoon vanilla extract

½ teaspoon ground cinnamon

¼ teaspoon kosher salt

¾ cup chopped pecans

2 cups mini marshmallows

9 Mini-Puft heads (page 59)

ADDITIONAL SUPPLIES

Kitchen torch

1. Preheat the oven to 350°F. Grease a 2-quart baking dish with nonstick spray.

2. Bring a large pot of water to a boil. Add the sweet potatoes and cook for 16 to 18 minutes, until fork tender. Drain.

3. Place the hot sweet potatoes in a large bowl. Add the heavy cream, butter, brown sugar, maple syrup, vanilla, cinnamon, and salt. With an electric handheld mixer on low speed, mash until combined. Spread the mixture into the prepped baking dish. Sprinkle on the pecans, then bake for 20 minutes.

4. Spread the mini marshmallows evenly on top. Place the mini-puft heads around the top of the casserole. Torch to serve.

LOUIS'S NUTRITIOUS QUINOA SALAD

DIFFICULTY: Easy	YIELD: 6 servings	PREP TIME: 15 minutes	COOK TIME: 15 minutes	DIETARY: GF, V, V+

WINSTON ZEDDEMORE: Used to be, quinoa wasn't known like it is today. In fact, I don't think it even hit the US till '84, maybe '85. I'd never heard of it, anyway—not until I took Louis Tully to lunch two, maybe three, years after we thought we'd busted the last ghost in the city. I was looking for some tax advice on starting a business of my own, and Louis was good enough to walk me through things. More than the advice, I remember the food; I had a steak, and Louis had some kinda salad, looked like it was full of couscous. That's when he told me about quinoa—health nut that he is, Louis went on for twenty minutes about the stuff before he remembered that he hadn't started eating yet, then asked for a to-go box. I had to take him to another lunch to get any advice out of him . . .

DRESSING

2 tablespoons olive oil

1 tablespoon balsamic vinegar

1 tablespoon lemon juice

½ teaspoon dried basil

½ teaspoon ground cumin

½ teaspoon dried oregano

¼ teaspoon kosher salt

¼ teaspoon ground black pepper

SALAD

2 cups vegetable broth

1 cup quinoa, rinsed

1 cup halved cherry tomatoes

1 cup diced cucumber

½ cup corn

½ cup diced red onion

3 tablespoons chopped fresh cilantro

1. To make the dressing: In a small bowl, whisk together the olive oil, balsamic vinegar, lemon juice, basil, cumin, oregano, salt, and pepper. Set aside.

2. To make the salad: In a small saucepan over high heat, bring the vegetable broth to a boil. Stir in the quinoa, reduce the heat to low, and cover. Simmer for 15 minutes, until the liquid has been absorbed. Fluff the quinoa, then cool for 10 minutes.

3. Spoon the quinoa into a large bowl. Add the tomatoes, cucumber, corn, onion, and cilantro, tossing to combine.

4. Pour over the dressing, and lightly toss to coat. Serve.

YES, HAVE SOME AMBROSIA

DIFFICULTY: Easy	**YIELD:** 8 servings	**PREP TIME:** 2 hours	**COOK TIME:** N/A	**DIETARY:** GF

PODCAST: We have another marshmallow recipe, and I refuse to talk about it, so I'm bringing in a guest. Lucky is one of the few people, along with myself, Mr. Grooberson, Phoebe, and the rest of the Spengler family, to experience the only interdimensional cross-rip ever seen in this part of Oklahoma, and the thing I want to know most is: How did you get your name?

LUCKY: You're not going to make me say, "Just Lucky, I guess," are you? Because if you are, stop recording now.

PODCAST: This isn't for MTUU—I mean, it could be, but it's really for something different. Have you ever heard of ambrosia? Tell us about it. Go.

LUCKY: The fruit salad? I guess I like the sweet-on-sweet and with the crunch of the apples. We had it at Spinners until someone caught the line cooks double-dipping in the supply. Now I only get it when my nana makes it for holidays. If she wants to show off, she adds extra coconut. Um, what is this interview about?

PODCAST: It's about coconut now. Mmmm.

1 Granny Smith apple, cored and diced

1 cup red grapes

1 (11-ounce) can mandarin oranges, well drained

1 (8-ounces) can crushed pineapple, well drained

8 ounces frozen whipped topping, thawed

½ cup vanilla yogurt

1 ½ cups mini marshmallows

½ cup shredded coconut

1 cup maraschino cherries

1. In a large bowl, toss together the apple, grapes, oranges, and pineapple.

2. Fold in the whipped topping, vanilla yogurt, mini marshmallows, and coconut. Refrigerate for 2 hours.

3. Garnish with the cherries to serve.

UGLY LITTLE SPUDS

DIFFICULTY: Easy	**YIELD:** 6 servings	**PREP TIME:** 15 minutes	**COOK TIME:** 40 minutes	**DIETARY:** GF, V, V+

PETER VENKMAN: So, it was our first call, right, the Sedgewick Hotel, and we don't know what to expect. The only other ghost we'd seen was a phantom librarian that had chased us halfway down Fifth Avenue, so we probably though the Sedgewick ghost would look like a person, too. Or, y'know, maybe a sheet. Instead, what we got, as Ray put it, was an ugly little spud. The thing was shaped just like a potato. With arms. And butt cheeks. And it had a real bad attitude, man. That was its real ugliness. So yeah, a green potato-shaped ghost. You can see how a recipe that adds spuds to chimichurri might call that to mind—and if you can't, I could probably explain. I do have a psychology degree sitting around somewhere.

POTATOES

3 pounds creamer potatoes

1 tablespoon olive oil

½ teaspoon kosher salt

¼ teaspoon ground black pepper

CHIMICHURRI

2 garlic cloves, peeled

½ cup fresh cilantro leaves

½ cup fresh parsley

1 tablespoon fresh oregano leaves

1 tablespoon red wine vinegar

1 tablespoon lemon juice

½ cup olive oil

½ teaspoon kosher salt

1. Preheat the oven to 400°F. Line a baking sheet with parchment paper.

2. To make the potatoes: On the prepared baking sheet, toss the potatoes with the olive oil. Season with the salt and pepper. Roast for 40 minutes, until tender.

3. To make the chimichurri: While the potatoes are cooking, in a food processor or blender, combine the garlic, cilantro, parsley, oregano, red wine vinegar, and lemon juice and blend until smooth. Pour into a large bowl.

4. Stir in the olive oil and salt. Add the potatoes and toss to coat.

5. Serve warm.

GHOSTBUSTERS SUPER DIET SALAD

DIFFICULTY: Easy	**YIELD:** 4 servings	**PREP TIME:** 15 minutes	**COOK TIME:** N/A	**DIETARY:** GF

JANINE MELNITZ: For a while, the Ghostbusters were so busy that the phone was ringing off the hook. I literally didn't have time to even think about taking a bite of the lunch that I brought, and it was starting to get a little expensive, if you don't mind my saying. But I got the last laugh. My friend Carla temped over at one of the tabloids and said all the magazines and newspapers and talk shows—they were looking for new angles on the Ghostbusters, and if I had a hot tip, I could make a little money. Now I would never betray a trust or spread gossip—that's just not the kind of person I am. But I am the kind of person who might suggest that the salad I didn't get a chance to eat for lunch that day was part of a special diet that kept the boys fit and healthy as they went from case to case. I made $500. It is a wonderful salad, however, and I do recommend it.

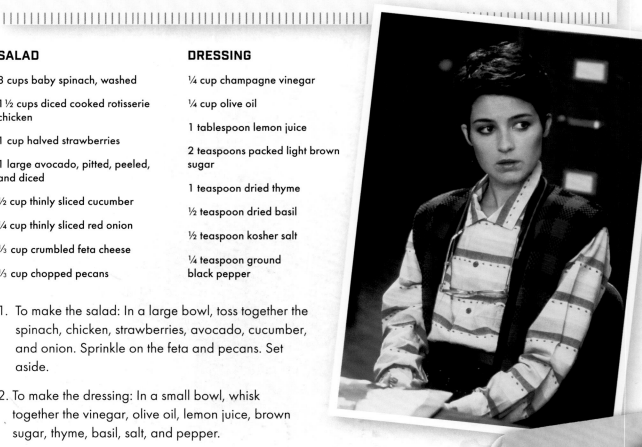

SALAD

8 cups baby spinach, washed

1 ½ cups diced cooked rotisserie chicken

1 cup halved strawberries

1 large avocado, pitted, peeled, and diced

½ cup thinly sliced cucumber

¼ cup thinly sliced red onion

⅓ cup crumbled feta cheese

⅓ cup chopped pecans

DRESSING

¼ cup champagne vinegar

¼ cup olive oil

1 tablespoon lemon juice

2 teaspoons packed light brown sugar

1 teaspoon dried thyme

½ teaspoon dried basil

½ teaspoon kosher salt

¼ teaspoon ground black pepper

1. To make the salad: In a large bowl, toss together the spinach, chicken, strawberries, avocado, cucumber, and onion. Sprinkle on the feta and pecans. Set aside.

2. To make the dressing: In a small bowl, whisk together the vinegar, olive oil, lemon juice, brown sugar, thyme, basil, salt, and pepper.

3. Toss the dressing with the salad to serve.

SPINNERS' LOADED ONION RINGS

| **DIFFICULTY:** Difficult | **YIELD:** 8 servings | **PREP TIME:** 1 hour | **COOK TIME:** 30 minutes |

PODCAST: Consider the onion, at home in the dark of the earth. Warm. Secure. Serene. Fully at peace with its place in the world and, yes, the universe.

It is ripped from the embrace of the soil, brought into the cold sunlight, and sent on to the kitchens of homes and restaurants around the world. If it isn't diced or chopped, its many layers are pulled from each other, leaving rings that never seem as whole apart as they do together. Why do the tears come? Because of their plight.

The rings are battered and seasoned, then fried in a vat of bubbling, sizzling, unforgiving oil. They become something more than what they were, and yet, something less.

Sorry. I couldn't think of anything ghost related, so I decided to practice setting the mood—you can't have a good show if you don't know how to set the scene.

Man, I am so craving onion rings right now. I should just go to Spinners and get some.

---

1 quart vegetable oil, for frying

¾ cup all-purpose flour

¼ cup cornstarch

1 teaspoon kosher salt

½ teaspoon garlic powder

½ teaspoon onion powder

½ teaspoon paprika

¼ teaspoon ground black pepper

¼ teaspoon ground cayenne

1 large sweet onion, sliced into ¼-inch rings

¾ cup buttermilk

1 large egg, lightly beaten

1 cup panko bread crumbs

1½ cups cheddar cheese

4 slices cooked bacon, crumbled

2 green onions, minced

1. Preheat the oven to 350°F. Line a baking sheet with parchment paper. In a Dutch oven over medium-high heat, heat the vegetable oil to 350°F.

2. In a sealable bag, mix the flour, cornstarch, salt, garlic powder, onion powder, paprika, pepper, and cayenne. Add the onion rings, and shake to coat. Remove the flour-coated onion rings and place on the prepped baking sheet.

3. Pour the remaining flour mixture into a shallow dish and whisk in the buttermilk and egg to make a batter. Place the panko in another shallow dish.

4. Dip the onion rings in the batter until coated, shaking off the excess, then dip them into the panko to coat.

5. Working in batches, place the battered onion rings in the hot oil. Fry for 2 to 3 minutes, until golden brown. Let drain on a wire rack.

6. Place the onion rings back on the prepped baking sheet. Top with the cheese and bacon. Bake for 10 minutes, until the cheese has just melted.

7. To serve, top with the green onions.

EGON'S FAVORITE MAC AND CHEESE

DIFFICULTY: Difficult	**YIELD:** 8 servings	**PREP TIME:** 15 minutes	**COOK TIME:** 40 minutes	**DIETARY:** V

PETER VENKMAN: There may not be any single human being on this planet that loves junk food as much as Egon Spengler. Seriously, I once got him to audit a course for me in his spare time in exchange for four bags of potato chips and a case of snack cakes.

That wasn't even the only benefit I got out of Egon's constant cravings—now, see, I'm a "bread crumbs on the mac and cheese" kinda guy. Call me a traditionalist, but there's gotta be some crust on there. Anyway, one night back in college, I got a sudden urge for the stuff, but there were no bread crumbs to be had—so I grabbed Egon's cheese crackers instead. Hit the spot, even if I only got one helping before Spengs descended upon the pan. Became one of his favorite things. But the important part? For the rest of the year, I impressed the coeds with my whole "thinking outside the box" vibe. That was an important lesson for me. Either way, it's good.

MACARONI

16 ounces elbow macaroni

4 cups shredded sharp cheddar cheese

1½ cups shredded Gruyère cheese

8 tablespoons (1 stick) unsalted butter

½ cup all-purpose flour

3 cups whole milk

1 cup heavy cream

1 teaspoon dry mustard

1 teaspoon garlic powder

1 teaspoon paprika

½ teaspoon kosher salt

½ teaspoon white pepper

TOPPING

2 cups cheese crackers, roughly crushed

6 tablespoons unsalted butter, melted

1. To make the macaroni: In a large pot over high heat, bring water to a boil. Add the macaroni and cook for 8 minutes. Drain but do not rinse.

2. In a medium bowl, combine the cheddar cheese and Gruyère. Set aside.

3. Preheat the oven to 350°F. Grease a deep 13-by-9-inch baking dish with nonstick spray. Set aside.

4. In a Dutch oven over medium heat, melt the butter. Add the flour and whisk for 1 minute, until lightly browned. Add the milk and heavy cream and whisk for 1 to 2 minutes, until bubbling.

5. Stir in the mustard, garlic powder, paprika, salt, and white pepper.

6. Set aside 1½ cups of the combined cheeses, then stir the remaining 4 cups of cheese into the pot, whisking until smooth.

7. Stir in the cooked macaroni, tossing to coat. Pour it into the prepped baking dish. Sprinkle the reserved 1½ cups of cheese.

8. To make the topping: In a small bowl, stir together the cheese crackers and melted butter.

9. Spread the topping evenly over the macaroni mixture. Bake for 25 minutes, until browned and bubbly. Serve hot.

TOASTED MARSHMALLOW SKEWERS

DIFFICULTY: Easy	**YIELD:** 4 servings	**PREP TIME:** 15 minutes	**COOK TIME:** 5 minutes	**DIETARY:** GF

RAY STANTZ: An underappreciated and vital component to supernatural investigations is a good sense of smell. No one tells you this as often as they should, but spectral presences, both benign and, more frequently, aggressive, can be detected by use of the ol' sniffer before even a PKE meter has the chance to pick it up. Like I said, that's vital. A wonderful training ground for olfactory prowess is cooking, of course, but not all cooking can be considered equal. For my money, skewered foods offer the purest scents, from the campfire roast of weenies and marshmallows to a savory selection of kebabs. Specifically floral scents pop up with the spirits of departed loved ones, but fruit, marshmallow, and sometimes chocolate are the general go-to scents used by a negative entity to sneak up on you, catch you with your guard down. No matter how much it may try to hide its darkness with a sweeter smell, the charring will poke through. These grilled-fruit-and-marshmallow skewers are a great way to train your nose to know the scent! (And as a bonus, they make for a great side!)

4 Mini-Pufts (page 59)

8 blueberries

8 cantaloupe chunks

8 pineapple chunks

8 strawberries

ADDITIONAL SUPPLIES

4 skewers

Kitchen torch

1. Place two pieces of each type of fruit onto the skewers, placing the mini-pufts in the center.

2. Use a kitchen torch to roast, then serve.

SLIMER SALAD

DIFFICULTY: Easy	**YIELD:** 8 servings	**PREP TIME:** 1 hour 15 minutes	**COOK TIME:** N/A	**DIETARY:** GF

RAY STANTZ: What this gelatinous concoction reminds me of is the class 5 free-roaming vapor that had haunted the Sedgewick Hotel. The little green pest of a ghost that, as Venkman noted in the archival material, I compared to an "ugly little spud." Whenever this disgusting blob would pass through solid matter—such as a wall, or Venkman—it would leave a healthy splatter of green ectoplasm in its wake that looked for all the world like green gelatin. When that little slimer got loose from the containment unit during the breach that preceded the first coming of Gozer the Gozerian, it didn't return to the hotel that had been its original stamping ground, but there were infrequent reports of it seen around New York that I've personally investigated over the years. I've yet to spot the beast, but I have occasionally seen evidence of its passing—often in the confines of the city's world-class public transportation system. (It likes buses.) The best and frequently only way I can discern the difference between this ghost's ectoplasmic discharge and a spilled dessert is whether or not it smells like feet. Take that for what you will.

1 (20-ounce) can crushed pineapple, drained

1 cup mini marshmallows

1 (3-ounce) package lime gelatin

½ cup chopped pistachios

2 cups frozen whipped topping, thawed

Whipped cream, for serving

8 maraschino cherries, for garnish

1. In a large bowl, stir together the pineapple, marshmallows, lime gelatin, and pistachios.

2. Fold in the whipped topping.

3. Spoon into eight serving dishes. Refrigerate for 1 hour.

4. To serve, top with whipped cream and cherries.

CHAPTER

4

SUPERNATURAL SWEETS

Here we are—desserts, the final course. As you may or may not know, the word is derived from the French word *desservir*, which roughly translates to "clean the table." Nuts, berries, honey, and assorted other treats are the sweet farewell to any meal, and well worth looking forward to. Myself, I always gravitated more toward good old-fashioned ice cream whenever I had the chance—but there are plenty of other fine possibilities, and we've curated a heckuva selection here. Take a look.

THAT'S A BIG TWINKIE

| **DIFFICULTY:** Medium | **YIELD:** 12 servings | **PREP TIME:** 25 minutes | **COOK TIME:** 30 minutes |

EGON SPENGLER: Under the best of circumstances, the typical amount of psychokinetic energy that should be in the New York area, or any major metropolitan area, remains at a consistent level. For purposes of this explanation, I'll use an example I used before to explain this concept to Winston: a Twinkie. On a normal day, the ambient PKE in a city this size would be roughly the size of that small prepackaged snack cake. But when you add a god-level entity into the mix, the PKE increases exponentially. During the approach of Gozer, the Twinkie in our example would weigh more than a quarter ton and be a little over ten meters long. As Winston said, "That's a big Twinkie." I'm not sure how the reiteration helps this cookbook project of yours, Venkman, but I find myself curious about just how large a Twinkie one might construct in a home kitchen. Perhaps I'll have to conduct an experiment and find out for myself . . .

CAKE

9 large eggs, room temperature

1½ cups granulated sugar

1½ cups cake flour

1 teaspoon baking powder

½ teaspoon kosher salt

1 tablespoon vanilla extract

FILLING

6 tablespoons unsalted butter, softened

¼ cup marshmallow creme

1 teaspoon vanilla extract

¼ teaspoon kosher salt

⅔ cup confectioners' sugar

1. Preheat the oven to 350°F. Line a 16-by-4-inch pan with parchment paper, then grease the paper with nonstick spray.

2. To make the cake: In the bowl of an electric mixer with the whisk attachment, whip the eggs and sugar for 5 minutes until thickened and thick ribbons of batter fall from the whisk.

3. Fold in the flour, baking powder, salt, and vanilla until just combined.

4. Pour the batter into the prepped pan. Bake for 30 minutes, until golden brown and a toothpick inserted into the middle comes out clean. Let cool for 20 minutes in the pan, then remove from pan and set aside.

5. To make the filling: In a large bowl with an electric handheld mixer set on medium speed, beat the butter, marshmallow creme, vanilla, and salt.

6. Add the confectioners' sugar and continue beating until smooth. Place into a piping bag.

7. Use a large dowel or straw to space 4 to 5 holes on the bottom of the cake, being careful not to penetrate all the way through. Pipe the filling into the holes, ¾ full. Carefully turn the cake over.

8. Slice to serve.

LUCKY'S DONUTS

| **DIFFICULTY:** Medium | **YIELD:** 24 donut holes | **PREP TIME:** 10 minutes | **COOK TIME:** 15 minutes | **DIETARY:** V |

PODCAST: We're talking again with my friend Lucky, the only daughter of the town sheriff. Lucky, do you think that, in the deepest levels of the collective consciousness—you know, the place that most people can only access indirectly on, like, an instinctual level because it's where the Illuminati openly communicate with the lizard people—do you think there's a mystic convergence that touches us all and leads us into cliches? Like, how cops like donuts?

LUCKY: Everyone likes donuts. I don't think the collective . . . whatever has anything to do with that.

PODCAST: But can you explain why cops like donuts?

LUCKY: . . . Because sugar tastes good?

PODCAST: Nice try, but it's totally the collective consciousness, which you can find out about in episodes sixty-eight through seventy-three of *Mystical Tales of the Unknown Universe* . . .

DONUTS

2 cups all-purpose flour

¼ cup granulated sugar

1 tablespoon baking powder

¼ teaspoon ground cinnamon

¼ teaspoon kosher salt

1 large egg

1 cup buttermilk

1 teaspoon vanilla extract

4 cups vegetable oil, for frying

COATING

⅓ cup granulated sugar

1 tablespoon ground cinnamon

1. To make the donuts: In a large bowl, whisk together the flour, sugar, baking powder, cinnamon, and salt.

2. Make a well in the center of the flour mixture. Stir in the egg, buttermilk, and vanilla, until just combined.

3. In a Dutch oven over medium heat, heat the vegetable oil to 350°F.

4. Working in batches, drop the batter by tablespoons into the oil. Cook for 3 minutes on each side, until golden brown. Let drain on a wire rack.

5. To make the coating: In a small bowl, stir together the sugar and cinnamon.

6. While still warm, roll the donuts in the mixture. Serve immediately.

1. In a medium bowl, whisk together the flour, baking powder, and salt. Set aside.

2. In the bowl of an electric stand mixer fitted with the paddle attachment, cream the butter and sugar until fluffy, about 5 minutes.

3. Add the egg and whisk until combined, then stir in the vanilla and blue food coloring.

4. With the mixer on low speed, slowly mix in the flour mixture. Once the dough pulls away from the sides of the mixer, the dough is ready. Divide the dough into two pieces and wrap them in plastic wrap. Chill for 30 minutes.

5. Preheat the oven to 350°F. Line 2 baking sheets with silicone baking mats or parchment paper.

6. Roll out the dough to a ½-inch thickness. Use the template to cut out three cookies. (Three cookies will be stacked to make one whole cookie.) Place them on the baking sheet. Leave the first one as is; this is the base cookie (cookie 1).

7. For the second cookie, cut a hole out of the center for the belly area. This is the middle cookie, which will be filled later (cookie 2).

8. On the third cookie, cut out the belly area, just as you did with the second cookie—but fill this one with the crushed candy powder. Press evenly so that it reaches all the sides of the cutout. On this same cookie, use leftover dough to create Muncher's eyebrow and face details (cookie 3).

9. Bake for 10 minutes. Let the cookies cool on the baking sheet, then transfer to a wire rack to cool completely.

10. Once cooled, use icing to stack the hollow cookie 2 onto base cookie 1. Fill the center with the sprinkles and fondant pieces.

11. Use icing to stack cookie 3 (with the clear center) onto cookie 2, enclosing the sprinkles between the top and bottom cookies.

12. Use black and white icings to create Muncher's face details.

13. With kitchen shears, cut a mini marshmallow in half. Onto each half, make two to three small cuts to create the fingers. Use icing to secure them onto the cookie. Repeat for all six hands.

14. Once the icing is set, the cookies are ready to serve. Break open the cookies to reveal the sprinkles inside.

CAMP WACONDA S'MORES COOKIES

DIFFICULTY: Medium	YIELD: 40 cookies	PREP TIME: 20 minutes	COOK TIME: 15 minutes

RAY STANTZ: Camp Waconda was a slice of Midwestern heaven, a place where one could go to learn things like canoeing or archery or the fine tradition of macaroni art. For me, the ghost stories heard around the campfire while we roasted Stay Puft marshmallows for s'mores is one of the many events that spurred my lifelong interest in the paranormal; I also saw a wendigo lurking in the woods north of the camp's lake. Add those things to the regular paranormal occurrences on the eastern seaboard of these United States and you wind up with a lifelong love of parapsychology that has yet to show any signs of faltering. Now, s'mores are key in the telling of a proper scary story, and I thought that we should say so. I imagined the correct ratio of graham cracker to chocolate to marshmallow (which is 2:2:1) would be emphasized. Instead, this recipe was dug up and presented. I was skeptical, but I'm not the type of person that skepticism persists in—one taste told me these cookies are a worthy substitute for those who can't get a roaring campfire going in their own neck of the woods. That said, ghost stories are still essential, and on that, I will not budge.

2 cups all-purpose flour

1 cup graham cracker crumbs

1 cup rice cereal

1 teaspoon baking soda

½ teaspoon kosher salt

1 cup (2 sticks) unsalted butter, softened

1 cup packed light brown sugar

½ cup granulated sugar

2 large eggs

1½ teaspoons vanilla extract

½ cup semisweet chocolate chips

½ cup mini semisweet chocolate chips

1½ cups mini marshmallows

1. Preheat the oven to 350°F. Line baking sheet with parchment paper.

2. In a medium bowl, whisk together the flour, graham cracker crumbs, rice cereal, baking soda, and salt. Set aside.

3. In the bowl of an electric stand mixer fitted with the paddle attachment, cream the butter, brown sugar, and granulated sugar on medium speed for 3 to 4 minutes, until fluffy.

4. Turn the mixer to low and stir in the eggs and vanilla until combined. With the mixer on low, add in the flour mixture until just combined.

5. Fold in the chocolate chips and mini chocolate chips.

6. Drop by large tablespoonfuls onto the prepped baking sheets.

7. Bake for 9 minutes. Remove from the oven and press three mini marshmallows into each cookie. Return to the oven and cook for another 3 minutes, until golden brown. Let cool on a wire rack, then serve.

DIRT FARM TRAP PUDDING CUPS

DIFFICULTY: Easy	**YIELD:** 6 servings	**PREP TIME:** 1 hour	**COOK TIME:** 5 minutes	**DIETARY:** V

PHOEBE SPENGLER: I didn't believe in the afterlife, or ghosts, at all. But science is about revising your beliefs after you get new information, and now that I know there are ghosts, I want to know as much as I can. My grandfather left behind a ton of books and writings on the subject. One, called *Tobin's Spirit Guide*, had a lot of notes in the margins, so I figured it was the most important and read it during the rest of summer school. A point that I found interesting in *Tobin's*, and one that was highlighted in marker, was that ghosts have the same type and level of sensory perception as we do. That's why my grandfather used his farm's empty field to hide hundreds of ghost traps—the loose dirt wasn't enough to keep the trap from operating, but it was more than enough to keep ghosts from noticing until it was too late. It was so simple a solution, I don't think I would have ever thought of it—but Egon Spengler was a genius. This recipe pays tribute to his plan in a unique way, using pudding cups to represent the field of hidden traps. Since I'm told my grandfather loved chocolate, I can only conclude he would have approved.

2 ounces dark chocolate candy melts

2 ounces yellow candy melts

1 (3.9-ounce) box instant chocolate pudding

2 cups whole milk, cold

8 ounces frozen whipped topping, thawed

1 cup crushed chocolate sandwich cookies

1. Line a quarter baking sheet with parchment paper. Set aside.

2. In a small microwave-safe bowl, melt the dark chocolate candy melts for 30 seconds, then for two 15-second intervals. Stir until melted and smooth. Set aside. Do the same for the yellow candy melts.

3. Place the melted candy into piping bags or use a spoon to draw alternating stripes of brown and yellow onto the prepped baking sheet. Refrigerate for 30 minutes, until solid. Cut into six small rectangles. Set aside.

4. Meanwhile, in a large bowl, using an electric handheld mixer, beat the pudding and milk for 2 minutes, until combined. Let stand for 5 minutes.

5. Fold in the whipped topping.

6. Spoon into six parfait glasses. Top with the crushed cookies. Refrigerate for 1 hour.

7. Place a piece of striped chocolate into the center of each one, then serve.

MR. GROOBERSON'S NIGHTMARE ICE CREAM SUNDAE

DIFFICULTY: Easy	**YIELD:** 1 serving	**PREP TIME**: 10 minutes	**COOK TIME:** N/A

GARY GROOBERSON: Is this still—are you still recording? I don't have any more thoughts on shrimp. Or cheese. But if you'd like to talk movies . . .

PODCAST: Actually, I wanted to ask where you were when you got possessed by the Keymaster.

GARY GROOBERSON: Oh! Oh. Well, you know, it's all a little fuzzy, but if I think hard . . . I was at the store, grabbing some ice cream. I was in the mood for a sundae, and—you know, that's the funny thing about sundaes. They're always kind of appropriate. Did you have a good day? Congrats, have a sundae to celebrate! Did you have a bad day? Too bad, console yourself with a sundae. Did your date's kids take out half of downtown Summerville with a particle accelerator? That's crazy—get a sundae. It really is pretty versatile, when you think about it.

PODCAST: So, you got a sundae.

GARY GROOBERSON: No, I got turned into a dog. Well, not at first. But I still ate just . . . a lot of kibble.

PODCAST: Sounds like you could use a sundae right now.

GARY GROOBERSON: You have no idea.

1 ½ cups coffee ice cream

¼ cup hot fudge

⅓ cup whipped cream

¼ cup mini marshmallows

1 tablespoon sliced almonds

1 You've Earned It Candy Bar (page 81)

1 Mini-Puft head (page 59)

1 maraschino cherry

1. Scoop the ice cream into a sundae glass.

2. Top with the hot fudge, then the whipped cream.

3. Sprinkle on the mini marshmallows and almonds.

4. Top with the candy bar, mini-puft head, and cherry, then serve.

PSYCHOMAGNOTHERIC SLIME-FILLED TOASTER TARTS

DIFFICULTY: Medium	YIELD: 6 servings	PREP TIME: 20 minutes	COOK TIME: 15 minutes	DIETARY: V

RAY STANTZ: It's a myth that all slime is a green, smelly ectoplasmic discharge rife with psychokinetic energy. Though green slime is the most common type, there are several others, each with a different chemical structure and defining properties. At one point, Egon and I sterilized a sample of slime and noticed it had kind of a sweet smell to it, and its consistency was something like jelly or marmalade—so, naturally, we experimented with consumption. I think I might have seen through time and space, which I do not recommend. That said, it tasted a lot like strawberries and cream, if you can believe it. If the sterilization process wasn't so difficult, this would make one heck of a pastry filling. Until then, good ol' fashioned jam will have to do.

TARTS

2 rolls refrigerated pie dough

1 cup strawberry jam

1 large egg

1 tablespoon water

ICING

1 cup confectioners' sugar

1½ tablespoons whole milk

¼ teaspoon clear vanilla extract

1 drop pink food coloring

1 tablespoon sprinkles

1. Preheat the oven to 400°F. Line a baking sheet with parchment paper.

2. To make the tarts: Unroll the dough and cut into twelve 5-by-3-inch rectangles. Place six of the rectangles onto the prepped baking sheet. Place about 2½ tablespoons of jam onto each rectangle.

3. Place the remaining rectangles on top of the jam, using the tines of a fork to press the edges and seal them.

4. In a small bowl, whisk together the egg and water to make an egg wash. Brush it onto the tarts.

5. Bake for 15 minutes, until golden brown. Let cool on a wire rack.

6. To make the icing: In a small bowl, whisk together the confectioners' sugar, milk, and vanilla. Stir in the pink food coloring until combined.

7. Spread the icing onto the tarts. Add sprinkles, then serve.

PHOEBE'S SPECTRAL CHESSBOARD CAKE

DIFFICULTY: Difficult	**YIELD:** 12 servings	**PREP TIME:** 1 hour	**COOK TIME:** 1 hour	**DIETARY:** V

PHOEBE SPENGLER: I said before that I didn't believe in ghosts. I didn't think it was rational, but my grandfather showed me otherwise with a game of chess. He was dead at the time. And invisible, which is something else I didn't think was plausible. We didn't ever finish our game, but we bonded in other ways; he silently showed me his workshop and how to repair the ghost-trapping equipment he designed. It was kind of nice just being listened to by someone who understood me. I still wish we'd been able to play our game to the end, and I think about what my strategy would've been every time I see a chessboard pattern—even the interior of this cake. (I believe I could've had checkmate in twelve moves.)

VANILLA CAKE

2½ cups sifted all-purpose flour

2 teaspoons baking powder

¼ teaspoon kosher salt

1 cup (2 sticks) unsalted butter

2 cups granulated sugar

3 large eggs

1 tablespoon vanilla extract

1 cup buttermilk

CHOCOLATE CAKE

2½ cups sifted all-purpose flour

½ cup unsweetened cocoa powder

1½ teaspoons baking powder

½ teaspoon baking soda

¼ teaspoon kosher salt

1 cup (2 sticks) unsalted butter

2 cups granulated sugar

3 large eggs

2 teaspoons vanilla extract

1 cup buttermilk

FROSTING

1½ cups (3 sticks) unsalted butter, softened

6 cups sifted confectioners' sugar

½ cup unsweetened cocoa powder

¼ teaspoon kosher salt

1 teaspoon vanilla extract

4 to 5 tablespoons heavy cream

GARNISH

2 tablespoons unsweetened cocoa powder

1 tablespoon confectioners' sugar

1. Preheat the oven to 350°F. Line four 9-inch round pans with parchment paper, then grease with nonstick spray.

2. To make the vanilla cake: In a large bowl, whisk together the flour, baking powder, and salt. Set aside.

3. In the bowl of an electric stand mixer fitted with the paddle attachment, cream the butter and sugar on medium speed for 2 to 3 minutes, until fluffy. Turn down the mixer to low, stir in the eggs and vanilla and mix until just combined.

4. With the mixer on low speed, alternate adding the flour mixture and the buttermilk, mixing until the batter just comes together.

5. Pour the vanilla batter into two of the prepped cake pans. Bake for 25 to 30 minutes, or until a toothpick inserted into the center comes out clean. Let cool.

6. To make the chocolate cake: In a large bowl, whisk together the flour, cocoa powder, baking powder, baking soda, and salt. Set aside.

7. In the bowl of an electric stand mixer fitted with the paddle attachment, cream the butter and sugar on medium speed for 2 to 3 minutes, until fluffy. Turn the mixer to low and add the eggs and vanilla and mix until just combined.

8. With the mixer on low speed, alternate adding the flour mixture and the buttermilk, until the batter just comes together.

9. Pour the chocolate batter into the two remaining prepped cake pans. Bake for 25 to 30 minutes, or until a toothpick inserted into the center comes out clean. Let cool.

10. Once the cakes have cooled completely, remove them from the pans and discard the parchment. Slice a thin layer off the top of the cakes to create a flat surface.

11. Place a 7-inch plate on top of a cake and cut around it to create a smaller circle. Then place a small 3-inch bowl in the center, cutting around that to create another small circle. Do this for all four cake layers. Set aside.

12. To make the frosting: In the bowl of an electric stand mixer fitted with the paddle attachment, beat together the butter, confectioners' sugar, cocoa powder, vanilla, and salt, until just combined. Add the cream, then whip for 3 to 4 minutes, until fluffy.

13. Place an outside chocolate ring on a serving stand. Insert a small vanilla cake ring, then the smallest chocolate piece. Frost the top. Place an outside vanilla ring on top, inserting a small chocolate cake ring, then the smallest vanilla piece. Continue stacking and frosting with the remaining cakes, alternating the color of the outer rings.

14. Once stacked, frost the entire cake. Refrigerate for 1 to 2 hours.

15. To garnish: Dust the top with cocoa powder, then confectioner's sugar. Slice to serve.

BUG EYE GHOST BLACKBERRY TARTS

| **DIFFICULTY:** Medium | **YIELD:** 6 servings | **PREP TIME:** 1 hour | **COOK TIME:** 10 minutes | **DIETARY:** V |

PODCAST: Okay, so, this kid from my class was drawing a ghost he swore flew past his house one night. It had an eye that popped out of its head—not like a zombie's that hangs down all gross, but, like, out of the top, like a balloon. The bug-eye ghost he drew seemed really familiar, so I researched it with some books Ray recommended. Now I'm 99 percent sure that it's either a pre-Atlantean battle-curse spirit, the kind of thing that was sent after your enemies if you got killed, or the ghost of a Kansas City basketball fan who spontaneously combusted when his team missed a winning shot back in the ancient days of 1972. I can't figure it out. Ray says that the journey of research is its own reward, and I'll know when I know. Until then, that ghost is living rent-free in my head. Even the blackberry tarts in this recipe look like ol' Bug Eye!

CRUST

1½ cups graham cracker crumbs

2 tablespoons packed light brown sugar

¼ teaspoon kosher salt

4 tablespoons unsalted butter, melted

FILLING

8 ounces blackberries

1 cup heavy whipping cream

6 ounces mascarpone cheese

¾ cup confectioners' sugar

2 teaspoons grated lemon zest

½ teaspoon vanilla extract

¼ teaspoon kosher salt

TOPPING

6 blueberries

6 peeled lychees, drained

Red food coloring

1 kiwi, peeled and cut into small 1-inch slivers

2 tablespoons slivered almonds

1. Preheat the oven to 350°F. Grease six 4-inch tart pans with nonstick spray.

2. To make the crust: In a medium bowl, stir together the graham cracker crumbs, brown sugar, salt, and butter. Press the mixture into the prepped tart pans.

3. Bake for 10 minutes, until browned. Let cool completely on a wire rack.

4. To make the filling: In a food processor, pulse the blackberries until smooth. Strain through a fine-mesh sieve and discard the seeds. Set aside the puree.

5. In a medium bowl using an electric handheld mixer, whip the heavy cream until soft peaks form. Fold in the blackberry puree, mascarpone cheese, confectioner' sugar, lemon zest, vanilla, and salt. Whip on high for 1 minute to thicken.

6. Spoon the topping into the tart crusts, using a spatula to spread evenly. Refrigerate for 1 hour, until ready to serve.

7. To top: Place a blueberry into the center of each lychee. Dip a toothpick into the red food coloring and add bloody stripes to the outside of each lychee. Place a lychee on top of each tart.

8. Add small pieces of kiwi below the lychee for the pair of eyes and slivered almonds for the teeth, then serve.

CHAPTER

5

PARANORMAL POTABLES

No matter what course is your favorite, you can't possibly have a meal without something to drink! Put the water aside and dive into this chapter, filled with beverages of every stripe. From hot to cold, sweet to refreshing, there's something to tantalize every taste bud—including the only class 5 free-roaming vapor you'll want anywhere near your taste buds!

MINI-PUFT HOT COCOA

DIFFICULTY: Easy	**YIELD:** 2 servings	**PREP TIME:** 5 minutes	**COOK TIME:** 5 minutes	**DIETARY:** GF

RAY STANTZ: Cocoa and hot chocolate have a fascinating history that goes back centuries. The Maya goddess Ixcacao and the god Ek Chuah were associated with chocolate and cocoa, respectively, and the drink the Maya prepared, the ancestor of our own hot chocolate, was mixed with corn, herbs, and sometimes blood, as it played a part in important rites within the society and in honor of the gods they worshipped. In more modern times, there was an occurrence in a Pennsylvanian chocolate factory in 1949. The manifestation first happened on October 20, which Spates' Catalog argues as the Gregorian calendar's equivalent of the start of the Mayan month of Muwan, when Ek Chuah is honored. Whether or not the math works out, what's true is that for twenty days, at approximately 1 a.m. each day, a solid minute of screams were heard emanating from the factory, culminating in several Maya glyphs being found smeared on the factory floor in melted chocolate. From November 9, 1949, until today, nothing similar has occurred. Was this a manifestation of one of Ek Chuah's followers, or the Maya deity himself? No one can say. But we still have hot chocolate, which remains delightful. I take mine with marshmallows.

1 cup whole milk

1 cup half-and-half

2 ounces semisweet chocolate, chopped

2 tablespoons unsweetened cocoa powder

2 tablespoons granulated sugar

½ teaspoon vanilla extract

½ cup mini marshmallows

2 Mini-Pufts heads (page 59)

ADDITIONAL SUPPLIES

2 umbrella picks

1. In a saucepan over medium-low heat, combine the milk, half-and-half, chocolate, cocoa powder, sugar, and vanilla.

2. Whisk and bring to a low simmer, then cook for 2 minutes, until smooth.

3. Pour the hot chocolate into two mugs. Top with the mini marshmallows.

4. Skewer the mini-pufts with umbrella picks and place them on top of the marshmallows, then serve.

GOZER'S COTTON CANDY COOLER

DIFFICULTY: Medium	**YIELD:** 2 servings	**PREP TIME**: 5 minutes	**COOK TIME:** N/A	**DIETARY:** GF, V, V+

RAY STANTZ: The concept of including a drink named after Gozer the Gozerian stretches all the way back to the '80s and our initial attempts to put together this cookbook—we simply couldn't see eye to eye on the kind of drink it should be. For my part, given that we are the Ghostbusters, I wanted to keep spirits out of the recipe. Peter disagreed, and that was that for the longest time. But I have learned that if you wait long enough, eventually, you'll get your own way—and with me largely in charge of this cookbook, that means we're left with a perfectly safe, perfectly tasty Gozer drink for everyone to enjoy in good health.

½ cup water

½ cup granulated sugar

½ teaspoon butterfly tea powder

1½ cups cold water

3 tablespoons lemon juice

3 tablespoons lime juice

Ice, for serving

3 cups cotton candy

1. In a small saucepan over medium-high heat, bring the water and sugar to a boil, until the sugar dissolves. Remove the simple syrup from the heat and let cool.

2. In a medium pitcher, stir together the cooled simple syrup, butterfly tea powder, and water. Pour into two glasses filled with ice.

3. Pour in the lemon and lime juices, stirring to change color.

4. Top with cotton candy and serve.

ECTO JUICE

DIFFICULTY: Easy	**YIELD:** 6 servings	**PREP TIME:** 5 minutes	**COOK TIME:** 5 minutes	**DIETARY:** GF, V, V+

PETER VENKMAN: Shortly after the ghostbusting thing really took off, I get this call from a fella in beverages. He says to me, "Pete, I want to be in business with the Ghostbusters." And I mean, hey, I love beverages. People gotta drink something. The guy had a whole strategy worked out: regional release followed by a limited national debut, a press tour, the whole nine. His team had whipped up some crazy drink that tasted like battery acid and sugar, they mocked up an ad for Ecto-Cola, there were T-shirts—and I'm sure you're asking, "Why haven't I seen any of this?" Because of my colleague Dr. Stantz, who decided in a shrewd move I didn't see coming to trademark the word *ecto*, refused to put the name on what he called "an inferior drink." So, the deal fell through, as they do. No hard feelings. But I'm calling this orange concoction Ecto Juice just to razz him a little. This drink is delicious and refreshing, and, best of all, it's orange—meaning you'll never confuse it for a glass of green slime by accident. (Trust me, that's a mistake you don't want to make!)

1 cup water

1 cup granulated sugar

3 cups orange juice (freshly squeezed, if possible)

1 tablespoon lemon juice

3 cups cold sparkling water

Ice, for serving

6 teaspoons grenadine

6 orange slices

1. In a small saucepan over medium-high heat, bring the water and sugar to a boil, until the sugar dissolves. Remove the simple syrup from the heat and let cool.

2. In a large pitcher, stir together the cooled simple syrup, orange juice, lemon juice, and sparkling water.

3. Place ice in six glasses, then pour in the juice mixture. Add 1 teaspoon of grenadine to each glass. Garnish with the orange slices, then serve.

THE KEYMASTER'S PEANUT BUTTER PARALLEL

DIFFICULTY: Easy	**YIELD:** 6 servings	**PREP TIME:** 5 minutes	**COOK TIME:** 5 minutes	**DIETARY:** GF, V

RAY STANTZ: Since a pair of complementary milkshake recipes are included in this book, my train of thought chugged down the track to another matched pair: the Gatekeeper, Zuul, and the Keymaster, Vinz Clortho. Where there's one, there's always the other.

PODCAST: Peanut butter and jelly makes you think of two horned dog monsters that possess people?

RAY STANTZ: There's also the art of dream interpretation, and the symbology of peanut butter—confusion and difficulty communicating—goes perfectly with the Keymaster, who seems to, in my experience, temporarily scramble the cognition of those it possesses. They're a little spacy during and for a short time after the Keymaster has control. As far as the flavor goes, there is no downside. I'm a dry roast crunchy man, myself, so I was pleased to see a crushed-nut topping as the bow on this drink. That said, if I was forced to choose between this shake and the Gatekeeper, I believe I'd opt for both. Peanut butter and jelly are meant to go together! The perfect synthesis of flavor.

1 cup chocolate ice cream

1 cup vanilla ice cream

3 tablespoons smooth peanut butter

½ cup whole milk

1 cup whipped cream

1 tablespoon melted peanut butter

2 tablespoons crushed honey-roasted peanuts

1. In a blender, combine the chocolate ice cream, vanilla ice cream, smooth peanut butter, and milk. Blend until smooth. Pour into a tall glass.

2. Top with the whipped cream. Drizzle over the melted peanut butter, top with the crushed peanuts, and serve.

THE GATEKEEPER'S STRAWBERRY SIMILARITY

DIFFICULTY: Easy	**YIELD:** 1 serving	**PREP TIME:** 5 minutes	**COOK TIME:** N/A	**DIETARY:** GF, V

RAY STANTZ: Ah, the strawberry. In many interpretations, it's an omen of goals about to be realized, but there's also a consistent connection to a feminine energy and agency, while jelly symbolizes clarity and insight. This is both opposite of and complementary to The Keymaster's peanut butter. Perfect description of The Gatekeeper.

PODCAST: You got all this from two random milkshake recipes? Why didn't we talk about dream stuff on my show?

RAY STANTZ: There's always next time. Oh! Strawberry shakes make me think of strawberries and cream, a distant relative of the concept of a berry-and-dairy treat. It was invented in the court of Henry VIII, whose ghost I once witnessed on a trip my senior year of high school. He stared up at me from the bottom of the Thames—I like to think that he was hiding from the lurking specter of Anne Boleyn. Anyway, I stand firm on my love for the complementary flavors of The Keymaster and The Gatekeeper together. Peanut butter and jelly really is my jam.

PODCAST: I hate not knowing if a pun was on purpose or not.

2 cups strawberry ice cream

½ cup frozen strawberries

½ cup whole milk

1 cup whipped cream

1 tablespoon melted strawberry jam

1 strawberry, for garnish

1. In a blender, combine the strawberry ice cream, frozen strawberries, and milk. Blend until smooth. Pour into a tall glass.

2. Top with the whipped cream. Drizzle over the strawberry jam. Garnish with the strawberry, then serve.

CLASS 5 FREE-ROAMING VAPOR CIDER

| **DIFFICULTY:** Easy | **YIELD:** 1 serving | **PREP TIME**: 5 minutes | **COOK TIME:** N/A | **DIETARY:** GF, V, V+ |

RAY STANTZ: There are seven classifications with which to sort a spectral entity, and as a Ghostbuster, the most common variety that's crossed my path here in the city that never sleeps is, in fact, the class 5. One of the most versatile and variable ghosts in both appearance and temperament, a class 5 couldn't be mistaken for a human being by any stretch of the imagination, but it'll often have human features or impulses. A recurring trait seems to be an incredible thirst, though liquid passes through their vaporous form like it would through a sieve. Still, they seem to enjoy the feeling of refreshing themselves, so if you happen to catch an autonomous apparition in your immediate area, consider distracting the beast with this pleasant beverage to keep it from any destructive impulses it may have, and then give us a call.

1 lime wedge

2 teaspoons green popping candy

1 cup ice

1 cup sparkling apple cider

¾ cup zero-sugar green apple sports drink

1. Run the lime around the rim of a tall glass. Shake the popping candy onto a flat dish and turn the glass over, twisting the rim into the popping candy.

2. Turn the glass back over and add the ice. Pour in the sparkling apple cider. Top with the green apple sports drink, then serve.

DATE NIGHT BOBA FIZZ

DIFFICULTY: Difficult	**YIELD:** 1 serving	**PREP TIME:** 1 hour	**COOK TIME:** 30 minutes	**DIETARY:** GF, V, V+

GARY GROOBERSON: And this is the last interview? Because I really should probably be doing something productive.

PODCAST: Like looking for another old-school horror tape to show in class?

GARY GROOBERSON: Hey, now, that's not for every day—well, in summer school it is. But when the regular school year starts back up, it won't be more than twice a week. Is that all you have to ask about?

PODCAST: Actually, I wanted to ask about the cat mug on your desk that smells like mint. Why is the smell so strong? Is it to ward off evil spirits? Or is there another purpose? Are you an alien using the mint to mask the smells of human beings while you study us? And why does that mug look so much like the one from the restaurant downtown?

GARY GROOBERSON: What? You know I'm not an alien, Podcast, come on. You gotta get outside, dig into some hard science. Maybe get away from the paranormal stuff for a second.

PODCAST: And what about the mug?

GARY GROOBERSON: I . . . won it. Because I order at least two rounds of Lucky Cats every time I go to the—hey! I don't have to explain myself to you! You're twelve!

½ cup water, divided

½ cup packed light brown sugar

½ cup granulated sugar

¼ cup boba pearls

¼ cup lychees in syrup

1 teaspoon grated lemon zest

2 sprigs fresh mint, divided

12 ounces sparking water

1. In a small saucepan over high heat, bring 1 cup of water, the brown sugar, and the granulated sugar to a boil. Cook for 2 minutes, until the sugars have dissolved. Remove the simple syrup from the heat and let cool.

2. In a large saucepan over high heat, bring the remaining 2½ cups of water to a boil. Add the boba and reduce the heat to low. Simmer for 25 minutes. Remove from the heat, cover the saucepan, and let sit for another 25 minutes.

3. Drain and rinse the boba, then pour the boba into the cooled simple syrup. Let soak for 30 minutes.

4. In a glass, muddle the lychee, lemon zest, and half of the mint.

5. Drain the boba and spoon it into the glass.

6. Pour in the sparkling water. Garnish with the remaining mint and serve.

ZEDDEMORE EXECUTIVE COFFEE

DIFFICULTY: Easy	**YIELD:** 1 serving	**PREP TIME:** 5 minutes, plus 2 hours to freeze	**DIETARY:** GF, V

WINSTON ZEDDEMORE: I can't let this book come to an end without including the recipe my executive chef uses for the affogato I enjoy at the end of every week. Take it from me—it's a lot better than a reheated cup of coffee with two sugars and a splash of cream! And before any of you youngbloods out there think to get smart and suggest this belongs in the dessert section, let me tell you—you're gonna change your mind after you've had one for yourself. Now, get on into the kitchen and make a cup! I promise you it's worth it.

5 ounces cooled coffee

1 small scoop coffee ice cream

2 ounces hot espresso

1 teaspoon dark chocolate shavings

1. Pour the coffee into a small freezer-safe dish and freeze for 1 to 2 hours, until slushy.

2. Spoon the frozen coffee into a glass. Top with the coffee ice cream. Pour over the espresso.

3. Sprinkle with chocolate shavings, then serve.

PODCAST'S SUMMERVILLE FREEZE

DIFFICULTY: Easy	**YIELD:** 2 servings	**PREP TIME**: 10 minutes, plus 8 hours to freeze	**DIETARY:** GF, V, V+

PODCAST: Hard research is the core of Mystical Tales of the Unknown Universe. I head out into the field, searching. Always searching. Trying to uncover the secrets that are hidden all around us. It's an unending job, and it makes me thirsty—so I head over to Phoebe's house and ask her mom to make me a Summerville Freeze. (I named it after the town so I could list it as one of MTUU's sponsors!) The only thing about the Summerville Freeze is that you need a blender to make it, and for some reason, everyone—even Phoebe—seems to think I'm going to cut my hand off. Which is ridiculous! I helped save the world—I'm not going to cut my hand off with a blender! How would that even work? Okay. Whoa. I'm getting a little worked up. I'd better cool down with another Summerville Freeze (proud sponsor of MTUU)!

2 (12-ounce) cans lemon-lime soda

1 tablespoon blue raspberry syrup

½ teaspoon clear vanilla extract

1. Pour one can of soda into an ice cube tray and place in the freezer overnight.

2. Place the soda ice cubes in a blender. Pour in the second can of soda, the blue raspberry syrup, and vanilla. Blend until slushy.

3. Pour into glasses to serve.

AFTERWORD

Okay.

You made it through this—the cookbook that took decades to complete. Good for you. Good for Ray. I'm feeling a new hope for humanity.

I know I, for one, hope you found so many new recipes to add to the rotation that you start to notice your clothes are getting a little tighter. It'll give us a chance to sell you on our next archive title, *Exercising with the Ghostbusters*.

Kidding.

I'd like to tell you I was surprised when Ray told me he'd unearthed this book and wanted to complete it, but nothing surprises me anymore—not even getting a call in the middle of the night saying that I had to hop a private flight to Oklahoma and help stave off the apocalypse one more time.

You're welcome for that, by the way.

Ray did put out feelers to see if I was interested in contributing to this book in a more substantial way, but I gotta tell you, his new little protégé had it wired. They had this thing put together before I could even respond to the email Ray sent, let alone decide if I wanted to write up fifty ways to love your lunchtime.

But I did offer to write this closing note because, like with that trip to Oklahoma, I'm always there at the end.

Now, go make a grocery run and roll up your sleeves. It's time to go back through this thing and find something new to make—and if you've made it all? Make it again.

Doctor's orders.

See you on the other side,

Dr. Peter Venkman

Beloved psychologist and educator, and probably
your favorite Ghostbuster

ACKNOWLEDGMENTS

JENN FUJIKAWA: To my mom, Alice Kawakami, who once dressed up like a Ghostbuster for Halloween by wearing a vacuum on her back in place of a proton pack. To Kyle, Tyler, and Mason Fujikawa, who ate every marshmallow dish put in front of them despite much hesitation. To my brother, Mark, who has been crossing streams with me since birth. To my own OGB, Mel Caylo, Chrissy Dinh, and Sarah Kuhn. To Troy Benjamin, my fellow Mini-Puft pal, who always answers the call.

To the courteous and efficient friends who are on call twenty-four hours a day to serve all my supernatural-elimination needs: Cheryl deCarvalho, Chrys Hasegawa, Liza Palmer, Robb Pearlman, and Mary Yogi. To Erik Burnham, thank you for coming along with me on this ride—we got one! To Ghost Corps, Sony Pictures, Eric Reich, Camila Clifton, and Nicole Toczauer for allowing me to create my dream of cats and dogs living together—mass hysteria! To Justin Eisinger: We came, we saw, we kicked this book's ass!

One last word of wisdom to my kids: When someone asks you if you're a god, you say YES.

ERIK BURNHAM: I would like to thank the Academy, y'know, just for being there. To Jenn Fujikawa, thank you for letting me share these pages with you and your work—and for introducing me to affogato. To Justin Eisinger, thank you for bringing me to play in this new-to-me corner of publishing. To Eric Reich, thank you for letting me have so much fun in the Ghost Corps sandbox. Thanks to everyone at Ghost Corps, Sony Pictures, and Insight Editions for the mountain of work they do, ensuring that projects like this can make their way out into the world. And finally, to my friends and family members, many of whom would be irritated to be singled out and none of whom I want to omit accidentally—I'll cover my bases by thanking you all, for everything, full stop. I wouldn't be anywhere without you. Don't gloat—it's unbecoming.

ABOUT THE AUTHORS

JENN FUJIKAWA is a lifestyle and pop culture author, content creator, and host. She is the author of multiple fandom-based books and has created content for Disney, Ghostbusters, Lucasfilm, Marvel, Amy Poehler's Smart Girls, and more. See more of her unique family dinners and geeky baking on her website, JustJennRecipes.com, and on Instagram @justjennrecipes.

ERIK BURNHAM was once convinced that he should be a magician, but with no manual dexterity, he instead gravitated to creating stories. He is best known for his long run writing for IDW Publishing's *Ghostbusters* comic. He calls Minnesota home, and you betcha—it's chilly there. You can find his website at www.burnhamania.com, or follow him on Twitter @erikburnham.

NOTES

_____

_____

_____

_____

_____

_____

_____

_____

_____

_____

_____

_____

MEASUREMENT CONVERSIONS

VOLUMES

US	METRIC
⅕ teaspoon (tsp)	1 ml
1 teaspoon (tsp)	5 ml
1 tablespoon (tbsp)	15 ml
1 fluid ounce (fl. oz.)	30 ml
⅕ cup	50 ml
¼ cup	60 ml
⅓ cup	80 ml
3.4 fluid ounces (fl. oz.)	100 ml
½ cup	120 ml
⅔ cup	160 ml
¾ cup	180 ml
1 cup	240 ml
1 pint (2 cups)	480 ml
1 quart (4 cups)	.95 liter

TEMPERATURES

FAHRENHEIT	CELSIUS
200°	93.3°
212°	100°
250°	120°
275°	135°
300°	150°
325°	165°
350°	177°
400°	205°
425°	220°
450°	233°
475°	245°
500°	260°

WEIGHT

US	METRIC
0.5 ounce (oz.)	14 grams (g)
1 ounce (oz.)	28 grams (g)
¼ pound (lb.)	113 grams (g)
⅓ pound (lb.)	151 grams (g)
½ pound (lb.)	227 grams (g)
1 pound (lb.)	454 grams (g)

*PUBLISHER AND AUTHORS NOT RESPONSIBLE IF AND/OR WHEN THE MINI-PUFTS COME ALIVE AND RUN AMOK. PLEASE CONTACT A REPUTABLE PARANORMAL INVESTIGATION AND ELIMINATION SERVICE IN CASE OF EMERGENCY.

INSIGHT EDITIONS

PO Box 3088
San Rafael, CA 94912
www.insighteditions.com

Find us on Facebook: www.facebook.com/InsightEditions
Follow us on Twitter: @insighteditions

ISBN: 978-1-64722-740-1

Publisher: Raoul Goff
VP of Licensing and Partnerships: Vanessa Lopez
VP of Creative: Chrissy Kwasnik
VP of Manufacturing: Alix Nicholaeff
VP, Editorial Director: Vicki Jaeger
Designers: Leah Bloise Lauer and Monique Narboneta Zosa
Senior Editor: Justin Eisinger
Associate Editors: Harrison Tunggal and Anna Wostenberg
Editorial Assistant: Sami Alvarado
Managing Editor: Maria Spano
Senior Production Editor: Elaine Ou
Production Associate: Deena Hashem
Senior Production Manager, Subsidiary Rights: Lina s Palma Temena

 REPLANTED PAPER

Insight Editions, in association with Roots of Peace, will plant two trees
for each tree used in the manufacturing of this book. Roots of Peace is
an internationally renowned humanitarian organization dedicated to
eradicating land mines worldwide and converting war-torn lands into
productive farms and wildlife habitats. Roots of Peace will plant two
million fruit and nut trees in Afghanistan and provide farmers there with
the skills and support necessary for sustainable land use.

Manufactured in China by Insight Editions

10 9 8 7 6 5 4 3 2 1